The Eddie Fisher Story

THE
Eddie Fisher
STORY

by
Myrna Greene

Paul S. Eriksson, *Publisher*
Middlebury, Vermont

Copyright © 1978 by Myrna Greene
All rights reserved. No part of this work may be reproduced or transmitted in any form by any means, electronic or mechanical, including photocopying and recording, or by any information storage or retrieval system, without permission in writing from Paul S. Eriksson, *Publisher,* Middlebury, Vermont 05753. Published simultaneously in Canada by George J. McLeod, Ltd. Toronto, Ontario.
Printed in the United States of America.

Library of Congress Cataloguing in Publication Data

    Greene, Myrna
      The Eddie Fisher Story

    Includes index.
    1. Fisher, Eddie. 2. Singers—United States—
    Biography. I. Title.
ML420.F513G7   784'.092'4 [B]   78-19867
ISBN 0-8397-8682-4

To all those who said, "Eddie Fisher!
Who'd want to write a book about Eddie Fisher?"

Contents

List of Illustrations, ix
Preface, xi
Introduction   Epitomizing the Fifties, 3
1   The Idol of the Fifties, 11
2   The Kid from South Philadelphia, 21
3   Sonny Edwards Goes to Town, 37
4   Creating Eddie Fisher, 51
5   Mr. Fisher Goes to War, 61
6   E-D-Die! (Or not a Dry Seat in the House), 69
7   The All-American Boy and Girl, 79
8   The Marriage that Almost Wasn't, 97
9   Trouble, 117
10   Triangles, 127
11   The Fallen Idol, 149
12   Ups and Downs with Uppers and Downers, 161
13   Eddie Who?, 181
Index, 203

List of Illustrations

The many faces of Eddie Fisher, 20
With Eddie Cantor and Jennie Grossinger, 34
Eddie's parents, Mr. and Mrs. Joseph Fisher, 35
Eddie and friends with Skipper Dawes and Eddie Cantor, 36
With Bernie Rich, Skipper Dawes, and Joey Foreman, 36
Young Eddie with Copa chorus girl, 74
With songstress, Jane Froman, 74
Kate and Joseph Fisher at Eddie's second Paramount opening, 75
Eddie with his brother, Alvin (Bunny)—1953, 75
Pfc. Edwin Jack Fisher, 76
Eddie with Francis Cardinal Spellman, 77
With Princess Margaret, 77
Bill Miller, Riviera owner, signing Eddie to contract, 78
Mr. and Mrs. George Montgomery (Dinah Shore) with Eddie, 78
With Al Jolson's widow and Harry Akst, 95
Eddie with Louella Parsons, 95
Two Aries personalities: Milton Blackstone and Debbie Reynolds, 96
Debbie and "Fanny," 111
Eddie and Debbie—Young love, 111
Eddie Cantor's engagement party for Debbie and Eddie, 112
Eddie's stepfather, Max Stupp, with his new family, 113

Newlyweds with Milton Blackstone and Jennie Grossinger, 114
Eddie and Debbie's wedding portrait—September 26, 1955, 115
The first Eddie Fisher family, 116
"Bundle of Joy" advertisements from
    RKO-Radio Pictures, 116
Mr. and Mrs. Mike Todd and daughter, Liza, 137
Eddie with second wife, Elizabeth Taylor, 138
Eddie with third wife, Connie Stevens, 165
Eddie's women: Barbara Hayman, Elizabeth Taylor, Debbie
    Reynolds, Connie Stevens, 166
Joan Wynn, 167
Terry Richard, 167
Some Eddie Fisher hits, 168
Eddie Fisher's children: Todd, Carrie, Joely and Tricia, 169
Mrs. Daniel Blackstone with Debbie after performance of
    "Irene," 170
Daniel Blackstone, Milton's brother, 170
Carrie Fisher in "Star Wars," 189
Bobby Hall, the murdered private detective, 189
Buddy Hackett, 189
Some newspaper headlines, 190
Eddie as he was . . ., 191
And as he is today, 192
. . . with Roy Radin's Vaudeville Revue, 193

Preface

Though Eddie Fisher may have brought about many of the problems in his own life, I truly believe he helped to save mine. For that, I am grateful.

I've always lived my life with the knowledge that God never closes one door without opening another. When I thought my life was possibly over, I found it was just beginning and that I would be given a look into a world far removed from my own sheltered existence in Central Pennsylvania.

Several years ago after a series of abdominal operations to correct the damage done from appendicitis not properly treated, I was told the unpleasant news I might have just one year to live. There would be little hope if surgery were required again during that time.

I had two choices. I could inflict my obvious fears and depressive moods on my husband and two small daughters, or I could enter into some project that would help me sustain my zest for daily living. I chose the latter.

In February, 1972, the day after a major Eastern snowstorm, my husband and I shoveled a path from our drive to a highway that led to the Holiday House, a popular nightclub in Monroeville, Pa., near Pittsburgh. Using a four-wheel-drive Jeep to make the

2½-hour trip, we continually fought snow squalls and snow drifts on the way to see the performer I once considered my idol.

As we drove, I recalled the first time I had seen Eddie Fisher. I was 12, Eddie was at the peak of his show-business career. My mother took me to New York where we stood in line for three hours in the downstairs lobby of the RCA Building waiting to be taken by elevator to see our hero. (Mother was a fan, too.) Exactly one minute before air time, Eddie made his appearance before hundreds of screaming females. This made quite an impression on a 12-year-old.

Already, he was too short for me, and he was so much richer than I. So dreams of Eddie Fisher whisking me away to never, never land were not part of my unending collection of material on the handsome singer who captured the hearts of women around the world.

That night in Pittsburgh, though, was quite different. I watched the aging baritone perform. He made sad jokes about himself and his ex-wives. His voice cracked and he looked physically like the one who had been told he had only a year to live.

At that time I knew nothing of Eddie's drug problems, but it was clear to me there was a story behind his face. I knew he couldn't look that haggard just because he had had several ill-fated marriages.

Driving home, it occurred to me that somewhere there remained boxes of my Eddie Fisher magazines, news articles, photos and fan club data. The search began.

It seemed my grandmother liked Eddie Fisher, too. Nestled in a dark corner of her attic was the missing memorabilia, exactly as it had been placed there years ago. Later she said, "I didn't think anyone would ever want it, but he was such a nice boy. I just couldn't destroy all those things about him."

Engrossed in the happy memories of my childhood, I didn't have time to feel sorry for myself. Still unaware of Eddie's private life, the idea of restoring Eddie Fisher to what I thought was his proper place in the entertainment world became an obsession with me. I wanted to renew my career as a writer, and I wanted Eddie Fisher to be the subject of my book.

I began by writing to Eddie's mother, his attorney, his booking agency—all to no avail. Reaching the President of the United States has to be an easier task than getting to Mr. Fisher. I was finally able to catch up with Eddie, but he had no interest in my cause.

Eddie, astrology oriented, was never pleased with the Aries (April 1) determination of Debbie Reynolds, nor the strong Aries (April 2) aggressiveness of Milton Blackstone. What he didn't know was that another Aries (March 31) was determined to write the story of his life, with or without his cooperation. Thus began the 3½ years of research that took me from coast to coast, the long-distance, collect phone calls at all hours of the day and night when someone remembered something about Eddie he had forgotten to tell me. Most of all came the six days a week of seemingly endless waiting for the mailman.

I never ceased to be somewhat nauseous every time Eddie did something that made news. I was always certain each particular thing could ruin the uniqueness of my whole idea. It never did. Instead, each incident only added to my story.

As the months passed, my health improved. A friendship with Eddie never developed, but my husband and I made many friends because of him. Among them, Milton and Daniel Blackstone.

Milton is one of the most impressive personalities I have ever met; he was also most cooperative as well as selective in the information he shared with me. My research made me aware of his strengths, but when I met him for the first time in 1975, he was physically drained. At that particular low period in his life he easily could have been bitter and blamed others for his misfortunes. But he never said an unkind word against anyone. He reminisced about all the good things he knew about people, especially Eddie. None of the material that made headlines concerning the physician, Dr. Max Jacobson, who was involved in Eddie's life from 1953-1966, was supplied by Milton, who has always considered him to be his friend.

Daniel Blackstone, Milton's brother, was always just a telephone call away and never asked for anything more than "truth" throughout the time I worked on the manuscript.

Paul Grossinger played host to my husband and me for several days at the resort while I delved into Eddie's "G" days. This made working on the book a pleasure.

I found talking to Mrs. Maxine Reynolds (mother of Debbie) a joy—a very gracious lady and a "star" in her kindness to others.

I talked also to family, friends, ex-friends, fans, secretaries, attorneys, accountants, musicians, physicians, dentists, celebrities, gays, straights, lovers, detectives, disc-jockies, wives, reporters, managers, body guards, go-fers, night-club owners, janitors, a rabbi and a priest. But at the risk of forgetting someone, I think it best to just say "thanks" to all who responded to my requests for bits and pieces of information about Eddie, and sometimes about Milton Blackstone.

I am especially indebted to James Neyland for his editorial assistance, guidance and suggestions, and to John Pickering, Editorial Director, University Press, Pennsylvania State University, who offered suggestions that helped make this book become a reality.

Much has been told about the fifties, but children of the seventies have been misled on many things that really happened. The early years saw love and romance blossom through the soothing words of love songs, sung by such popular singers as Eddie Fisher, Perry Como, Julius LaRosa, Patti Page, Joni James and Kitty Kallen.

Unlike what we see on the screen depicting life in the fifties, those who used four letter words were in a minority. Most romances did not take place in the back seat of a car. Rather, couples were content to hold hands, take walks and dance cheek to cheek at school dances or summer festivals. Young love was allowed to grow, sweet and uncomplicated. Eddie Fisher's rise to fame was part of that era. As the end of that decade ushered in the end of innocence and wholesomeness, Eddie's life style changed accordingly.

I've watched Eddie's star rise and fall and try to rise time and time again. To this day I believe Eddie Fisher to be one of the greatest singers of all time. If he ever makes it to the top again, I will be right there with a smile on my face, applauding.

The Eddie Fisher Story

Introduction—
Epitomizing the Fifties

It was midcentury, a turning point, a time for marking time. The 1950s didn't have an identity yet, but people talked about the twenties, the thirties, and even the forties with some assurance. The earlier decades of the twentieth century were easily identifiable by music, by fashions, and by attitudes. So then—the American people self-consciously assumed—would this sixth decade be identifiable. But how, they wondered, would it be?

For a people only recently out of a great depression and the most devastating war the world had ever seen, life had never been better. Affluence was something aspired to by everyone, and something achieved by many—if not by most, as the public press touted frequently. It was the century of sciences and progress—rapid progress. There seemed to be no limitations to human accomplishments.

Automobiles were being made bigger and better every year; a new invention called television was bringing entertainment into living rooms; and medical science seemed to be coming up with new wonder drugs and serums each year. New jetliners were making it faster, easier, and cheaper for Americans of all classes to travel, both within the country and abroad to foreign lands. By the end of the decade, both the United States and the Soviet Union would be sending rockets and satellites into space. People began to speculate, "Perhaps even the moon . . ."

Never had the country been closer to achieving the American Dream. All that was good and positive about the American character was obvious in the 1950s. Education and self-improvement were key words in the American way of life. Knowledge was power, and power was money, and money was what brought the American family all the good things it needed and wanted: the split-level or ranch-style house, the television set, the second car, the backyard barbecue, and the summer vacation.

Next to education and achieving the good life, Americans placed their greatest emphasis on generosity—on loving and helping neighbors. Of course, social critics in the 1950s had much to say about "keeping up with the Joneses" and "status seeking," but they ignored the vast amounts of money that had been pouring out of private pockets to help defeat polio, to help rebuild a devastated Europe, and to help build underdeveloped nations.

If Americans were beginning to lose some of their energy, their robustness, their naive charm, nobody seemed to notice. In fact, many Americans were beginning to look upon these qualities as negative ones. As more and more people traveled abroad, they were increasingly referred to as "ugly Americans."

Of course, there always have been flaws in the American character, and they were just as evident in the 1950s as were the good qualities. To some, they may have seemed more evident. The tendency toward self-righteousness led to witch-hunts that would cause the period to be called the "McCarthy Era." What had once been charming innocence and naiveté in the American character, in the fifties became a childish petulance and desire to be led by a great father figure.

The American public had always been inclined to admire and respect heroes—men and women of ordinary backgrounds who achieved greatness—whether it be a fictional Horatio Alger or a real Charles Lindbergh. In the fifties, this tendency was twisted into a kind of idolatry, creating demi-gods and mythological figures whose public images bore little resemblance to their private doubts and weaknesses. It was probably inevitable that these mythological creatures would eventually fall and bring about disillusionment, distrust, and lack of respect for what had once been positive values.

The 1950s in America can best be described as being much like the Roman god Janus, the god with two faces. Certainly it was a time of extremes, a time of oppositions. It might also be called a turning point.

The year 1950 did mark the end of the first half of the twentieth century and the beginning of the second half, and its significance was more than simply chronological. The opposing strains in all levels of life that had been conflicting seemed to meet in midcentury. On the economic level, capitalism and communism confronted each other in what was called the "Cold War." Pacifism and militarism met in Korea in what was called a "police action" to avoid the term "war." The more some people talked about "individualism," the more everyone sought refuge and security in groups of all kinds: unions, big businesses, social and political organizations, garden clubs, and fan clubs.

The more people became educated, the less able they found themselves to make their way in the world independently, using their own capabilities and resources. The more capable the people became, the more they found themselves dependent upon a centralized federal government and upon large businesses and corporations.

These were the strains of conflict and discord that would meet in the decade of the fifties, and be felt for many years afterward. These and one other: the conflict between the untried idealism and unbridled enthusiasm of youth against the staid and stable traditions of the older generation.

To many, this is the one characteristic that has most epitomized the 1950s. Certainly the fifties nostalgia that has surfaced recently has put an emphasis upon young people, their music and styles. Perhaps it is right to typify the fifties with its teenagers; certainly they were looked upon as a special generation from the very time they were conceived.

In the beginning, they were called "war babies," products of a "baby boom" that resulted from World War II. They were, many of them, children of soldier fathers and working mothers desperate to have families before it was too late. Because scientific knowledge was so important, these children were reared "scientifically" upon advice of pediatricians—and they also came to be known as the "Dr. Spock Generation." And because they were growing up, reaching their teens in record numbers in the 1950s, they came to be known as the "Rock 'n Roll Generation" as well. Partly because of their numbers, partly because of their own feeling of specialness, their impact would continue to be felt in the decades to follow. They would be the noisy, rebellious college students of the 1960s; and they would be the parents of the 1970s who would look nostalgically to their youth.

To epitomize the fifties nostalgically, then, it is appropriate to look back to the ducktail haircuts, the ponytails, the leather jackets, the bobby-sox and black loafers, the hoop-skirts, petticoats, and peasant blouses. It is also appropriate to epitomize it by its music—its crooners like Pat Boone and Eddie Fisher, and its rock 'n roll stars such as Fats Domino and Elvis Presley.

But the teenagers did not create the decade of the 1950s; they were merely responding to it. While their response is a very important part of what that time has meant to the United States, it is not the whole picture. More important than their response is what it was they were responding to. What they were responding to was a society that was changing so rapidly that its values, its mythology, and its reality did not always seem to match. Choosing which of these three to believe was a difficult—if not impossible—task.

American values were still supposed to be what they had always been—home, family, love thy neighbor; strive and succeed; set a goal and work toward it; with pluck and luck anyone could rise to the top in any field of endeavor. But rumblings had begun in the 1950s suggesting that these values were false, suggesting that the American Dream was an impossible dream. World War II left a legacy of bitterness and despair. The nihilism of the Beat Generation had begun to filter out to the young people—they called them Beatniks. And the intellectual weightiness of French Existentialism seemed to lend support to a new negative attitude that advised: live only for today; don't plan and strive, because there is no hope, there is no future.

The American mythology of the 1950s was one of excess. Automobiles couldn't look like autos anymore; they had to look like rocket ships so they sported tail-fins, a little bigger each year. With America's new importance in the world, presidents and politicians could no longer be ordinary men; they had to be of fatherly—if not heroic—proportions. If they could not be military men, then they at least had to be privy to secrets that ordinary citizens could not know. And the movie stars? Well, if they had been beautiful and exciting and glamorous before, they now had to be larger than life itself. With 3-D and Cinerama and Cinemascope and Vistavision, screen queens had to have bigger bosoms and redder lips and more perfect teeth than was humanly possible. The men had to be as pretty as—if not actually prettier than—the women; and they had to have unbelievable names like Rock and Tab and Troy. To match the mythology, the music, the dances, and the manner of dress had to be extreme as well. If the bobbysoxers of the 1940s had had fun, the kids of the 1950s were determined to outdo them and have more fun. Their music had to be louder, and their dances more outrageous.

It was the reality of the 1950s that was most difficult for young people or old to understand. The soldiers of World War II had returned home to find their country had changed almost beyond recognition. To mobilize for wartime, businesses had been given enormous concessions by government, including the underwriting of development of new products essential to the war. The government could not now forsake these businesses; it had an obligation to keep them operating and turning their products toward peacetime uses.

A new cooperation had also begun during wartime between union management and industry management, and that too continued after the war. The unions grew bigger and joined together to consolidate their power; businesses and industries did the same. The man who found himself without employment and outside the established order felt lost, as if facing an impossibly intricate maze. People still talked about "climbing the ladder of success," but for most in the 1950s (and afterward), the only thing they could do was to find a rung of the ladder and cling to it.

At any other time in American history, the middle-class working man might have rebelled; he would at least have elected leaders who would have been concerned about his concerns. But the 1950s were different, because the 1950s had something new called "Television."

The twentieth century had brought people many miraculous conveniences—automobiles, airplanes, telephones, radios, automatic dishwashers—but it is unlikely that any of these miracles had so profound an effect as did television. The new home entertainment acted like a drug; it allowed people to forget about their problems, to lose themselves in unreality. With television to come home to, people could accept the reality of their working day lives without protest. Television gave them the illusion of living well and living fully. It told them what they should want, what they should hope for, and what they should accept. And through its news coverage television gave people a larger reality to believe in, the reality of world events that superceded their own individual problems—communists lurking everywhere trying to overthrow the world.

Television also brought a great preoccupation with what came to be called "materialism." Because of the free enterprise system, the only way television could operate successfully and profitably was to have everything that appeared sponsored by business. And so the 1950s also became the decade of Madison Avenue, of hype and hoopla and whiter-than-white. Millions of homes across America tuned in their television sets every day or every night, demanding some form of entertainment or escape. That entertainment was paid for by soap companies and automotive manufacturers and drug companies. At no time in history had humanity heard more—or cared more—about tooth decay, bad breath, body odor, or dandruff.

However, the advertisers and their agencies did more than create a demand for their products. It was up to them to find the entertainment the American people wanted to see in their homes. And when they couldn't find the talent ready-made, the advertisers and the agencies had to manufacture it, at whatever the cost.

In the very beginnning, television didn't have time to develop its own stars; it had to borrow from movies, stage, nightclub, radio, record companies, and even newspapers. With the demand to produce something new every hour of every day, and with the heavy competition among the networks, the pressure was more than some entertainers could take, especially if their careers demanded that they make nightclub appearances or movies or recordings as well as their daily or weekly television show. Television had a voracious appetite, and it had the ability to consume entertainers whole if those entertainers did not have a superhuman energy, stamina, and endurance.

Some entertainers (and politicians) found ways of extending physical endurance beyond nature's limitations. The new wonder drugs worked miracles with human illness; it seemed logical that there might be drugs that could overcome human frailty as well. In the 1950s, it seemed that anything was possible through science and technology.

And so, quietly and secretively, what came to be known as the "drug culture" was born in the fifties. Of course drugs such as marijuana and cocaine and heroin had existed for years, but the 1950s provided medically approved uppers and downers and vitamin injections that seemed to be "safe."

Beneath the childlike innocence, beneath the chic and sophistication of stars and superstars, the 1950s planted the seeds of tragedy—a factor generally overlooked in considering the fifties.

What seems to epitomize the 1950s best is its stars—its actors and actresses, its comedians and singers. Like so much in the decade, they were larger than life; they were mythological figures. They were often figments of the fertile imaginations of managers, press agents, and sponsors; and so the reality of their lives rarely connected with their public illusions. They were products that were simply used to sell other products. As such, it was easy for managers, press agents, sponsors, and record companies to encourage their superstars to acquire super-energy through drugs and "vitamin" injections. It didn't matter if they should fall into a vicious circle of drugs for energy and drugs for sleep and drugs to counteract the drugs. At least, as long as the stars shone, they would shine brightly.

The necrology of 1950s superstars is almost endless—the most prominent names being Marilyn Monroe and James Dean. To many, these are the names that would most epitomize that happy and tragic decade, but they were not survivors. They were helpless victims.

Because the effects of the fifties survive, that decade can best be understood by viewing one of its superstars who still lives, one who epitomizes the best and worst that those years had to offer. The one who best fits those qualities is a star who shone brilliantly for the entire decade of the 1950s and then disappeared into all but oblivion. He was a sweet-faced young singer with a mellow baritone voice, and he seemed the epitome of everything that was good about the times. But he also fell prey to all that was bad.

His name was Eddie Fisher.

Eddie Who?

He is now all but forgotten, even by his most adoring fans. Occasionally, there will be the announcement in a gossip column that he is attempting a comeback, or there will be a picture of him in a tabloid looking bloated and dissipated, but most people cluck their tongues and go on to other things. They don't choose to recall that in the 1950s the name "Eddie Fisher" was a household word, that his records were at the top of the charts, that kids swooned at a glance, that he had everything that anyone could want—talent, money, fame, an adorable wife, and an adoring public.

As befits the American Dream, Eddie Fisher reached success despite humble origins. As befits the American values, he was good to his friends, to neighbors, and to strangers when he reached the top. As befits the fifties, he found himself caught in the role of a mythological figure, and he found himself strained beyond his human limits. Before the fifties were over, he would find himself torn between his private needs and his public image. Illusions and reality would be in conflict, and he would inevitably find himself caught in the vicious circle of drugs—first prescribed by a doctor with the explanation that they were "vitamin injections."

The legacy of the 1950s is not what nostalgic movies and television shows would have us believe—cute kids in leather jackets, chewing gum and talking funny. The legacy of the 1950s is, rather, what has happened to star and symbol Eddie Fisher in the years that followed the fifties.

1. The Idol of the Fifties

On April 10, 1953, a banner was raised above the marquee of the Paramount Theater in New York, announcing: "In person, EDDIE FISHER," and somewhat smaller below it, "Hugo Winterhalter and Orch." The movie playing was *House of Wax,* the first major motion picture in the 3-D process. Eddie Fisher was twenty-four years old; he was the top teen-age singing idol in the country. Although he had appeared at the Paramount before as an unknown supporting act, he was now teamed with one of the most important orchestras of the day, and he was being paid a sizeable $7,500 a week.

Opening night, he was showered with telegrams and flowers from family and celebrities. Eddie Cantor sent him an enormous floral wreath with a ribbon that read, "That's my boy." His mother sent a telegram saying, "To my Sonny Boy, wonderful son. Welcome home into civilian life. May God bless you and bring you all the luck and great success in your future life."

And, when the show was over, his mom, his old friends Joey Foreman and Bernie Rich, and his brothers and sisters were all backstage to greet him and congratulate him. All of them—parents, brothers, sisters, aunts, uncles, cousins, and friends—went to the famous Lindy's Restaurant to celebrate Eddie's fantastic success.

Eddie Fisher was packing the audiences in at the Paramount much the same way Frank Sinatra had done more than a decade before. Teenage girls were skipping school, bringing their lunches, and waiting in line for hours to see their idol. The lines outside the theater circled the block, the pictures and posters that advertised the appearance were smothered with imprints of lipstick kisses from his fans. Inside, when Eddie sang, they screamed, "E-d-die," and swooned.

Eddie loved it; he had realized his greatest dream. It had taken almost ten years, but he had done it. He was doing six shows a day, a grueling schedule, but he was so excited by it all, he felt he could keep going all day and all night. He had experienced the lowest of lows in his struggle to the top; now he was experiencing the highest of highs, and he wanted to savor the experience.

He was making a fantastic amount of money, and he was ready to spend much of it. For too long, he had had to watch his pennies. Now he went out and bought fine clothes—suits and shirts and ties and sweaters he had only dreamed about before. He also bought a car, a blue convertible, which he drove up to Grossinger's like the new star he was.

Despite the outward signs of good times and joyous relaxation, despite the impression nothing possible could go wrong with this new young singing sensation, Eddie Fisher was rapidly entering into a downhill course from the very moment he was on top. In the music business, getting to the top is only half the effort, staying there is the truly difficult thing. Being the most popular teenage idol in America requires constant exposure on television, on records, and in movies. And time becomes the idol's greatest enemy.

Within only a few days of his Paramount opening, Eddie also went into his new *Coke Time* show for NBC, and it too was an instant success. Eddie was the host of the show, which appeared twice a week; Don Ameche was his announcer, and Axel Stordahl led the orchestra. For each show, Eddie had a guest singer—Joni James, Perry Como, Vic Damone, Johnnie Ray, all of the most important performers of the time. Eddie, in turn, appeared as a guest on the important variety shows of Ed Sullivan, Dinah Shore, Perry Como.

Later in his career, Eddie would make a great many mistakes. However, in the very beginning, Eddie's mistakes were all selfless ones. He earnestly seemed to be trying not to let success go to his head. He must have realized the importance of his fans; how could he be where he was without them? He seemed to be doing everything he could to let them know he cared.

Eddie, like so many entertainers who reach "star" status, became surrounded by a protective army of employees. He already had famed Milton Blackstone, the great and powerful promoter, as his manager. Milton hired George Bennett, who had worked for him at Grossinger's, to be Eddie's public relations man when Eddie was at the Paramount. Later on, others would be brought in. However, during the Paramount days, Eddie's best friends—Joey Foreman and Bernie Rich—were often around, and they did their best to help out.

The phone was constantly ringing backstage; and, of course, everyone wanted to speak to Eddie. Milton or George Bennett or one of Eddie's friends would generally attempt to take the calls, to spare Eddie having to speak to the person. Once, however, the call was from a little girl who was seriously ill in a hospital. When he learned about it, Eddie insisted upon taking the call, saying, "Not Joey or George or the United States Marines are going to keep me from talking to this girl."

Eddie did see and talk to as many of his fans as his managers would allow, and he did try to do too much.

One young girl who managed to get close to him told him she was from London. Eddie was scheduled to appear there shortly at the Palladium. He asked if she intended to come to see him.

"I wrote to my mother," the girl told him, "and my sister, my aunt, and even my cousin. They can't get tickets; the Palladium is sold out both weeks you are there."

"Call me when I get over there," Eddie responded. "I'll take care of it."

"You can't," the girl insisted. "The place is sold out."

Eddie grinned. "Yes I can. You just call me."

Astonished, the girl asked, "Who do you know?"

Eddie almost always got his way, and he persisted in doing things against the advice of his managers. Inevitably, his overzealousness led to trouble.

It was a Saturday afternoon late one April, and raining hard. Despite the bad weather, Eddie's fans had lined up around the block of the Paramount, waiting patiently to get in to see Eddie. A cold wind was blowing the heavy rain, and whipping umbrellas and raincoats about. It was the kind of cold spring weather that can sink into your bones.

Eddie could see the fans out his dressing room window, and he was upset. "George," he accosted his public relations manager, "something's got to be done; they're going to get pneumonia."

George Bennett made the mistake of asking, "What can you do about it?"

Eddie thought for awhile, and then came up with an idea. He went to the window, opened it, leaned out, and tried to reason with the kids, telling them to go home. His fans were thrilled that he was speaking to them, and they would not think of going away to seek shelter. They kept up their banter for a good ten minutes, back and forth—Eddie asking them, pleading with them, to go away, and they responding that they were fine and would wait all day to hear him.

The longer Eddie kept his head out the window, the more upset George Bennett became. He kept trying to coax Eddie inside, but Eddie ignored him. Finally Bennett yanked him back in forcibly. When he had Eddie's attention, the PR representative started to berate him, "What do you think you're doing? Just because your legs are inside, you can't keep from getting a sniffle in your head." He implied that, just because Eddie's fans were fools, it didn't mean Eddie had to be one.

But Eddie was adamant. He shot back at Bennett, "Listen, if they think enough of me to stand out there, I'm going to take care of them."

Eddie had already been warned by his physician, Dr. William Hitzig, "If you don't rest between shows, you won't have any throat to be able to sing." George reminded Eddie of that warning, but Eddie wouldn't listen.

He came up with an idea. There was a rehearsal hall not in use, up one flight of stairs from Eddie's dressing room. Eddie called the Paramount management office and asked for permission to use it. Once it was cleared, Eddie set his plan into operation.

The backstage elevator at the Paramount had been installed for performers, musicians, and management; it would hold only eight people at a time; more than that would be too great a strain. Eddie insisted every kid be brought in off the street to wait for the next performance in the rehearsal hall. Eight at a time, the kids were ferried upstairs on the backstage elevator and guided into the rehearsal hall. Eddie went upstairs in his dressing gown and talked to the fans until showtime.

When he left, he said, "If you'll wait until I finish this show, I'll be back, answer your questions, and sign some autographs."

By seven o'clock that night, Eddie's head started to get congested and he began to feel achey. George Bennett sent for Dr. Hitzig, who came with plenty of penicillin and Vitamin C. He also demanded Eddie rest between shows, because his medication could achieve only so much by itself.

Eddie took his advice and lay on his couch sneezing.

George Bennett couldn't resist asking, "Are you sure there isn't something else you would like to jump up and do for those kids?"

Despite his cold, Eddie did not slow down enough to give his body and his throat an adequate rest. He continued to do six shows a day at the Paramount; he had recording sessions; he had his television show; he had guest appearances; and he had rehearsals for all of them. When it turned out Eddie needed an accompanist at the Paramount, there were also auditions. It was at one of these auditions Eddie took the most fatal step of his career—and of his life.

He had been warned numerous times—by Jane Froman, by Milton Blackstone, by George Bennett, and by Dr. William Hitzig—not to push his voice beyond its endurance. But Eddie would not listen to any of them.

On the crucial day at the Paramount, a young composer and arranger was auditioning for the position as accompanist. He was one of the best accompanists around New York, and he was hired. Eddie wanted to go into rehearsal immediately. Milton advised him to rest his voice for a few hours. But Eddie refused to take a break; he was excited about working and eager to get things moving.

Milton was angry about his singer's obstinacy, but he didn't want to start a scene in front of someone who had just been hired. So he shut up and let Eddie have his way.

Eddie talked to the accompanist for a short time about his arrangements and style. When the two seemed to be in agreement, they decided to proceed with the rehearsal.

As Eddie opened his mouth to start singing, nothing came out. His voice was completely gone. A look of fear and confusion crept over his face. He tried again. Nothing came out.

When Milton realized what had happened, he flew into a rage. However, he also realized it would do no good to shout at Eddie just then, so he walked out of the theater to allow the brisk spring air to cool his temper. He walked around the theater, and then went back inside, still not knowing what he could do for Eddie now that his voice seemed gone.

Once he got back inside, he found the new accompanist had a suggestion: there was a doctor who had helped a great many other entertainers with similar problems. Even politicians went to him. His name was Dr. Max Jacobson, and he gave special vitamin injections that would provide as much energy as any highly active person might need. His office was up on 86th Street, and he might be able to get Eddie back into shape in time for his next appearance.

Dr. Max Jacobson was one of the most highly respected physicians in New York in the 1950s. He was the celebrated doctor to celebrated patients—Cecil B. DeMille, Otto Preminger, Nelson Rockefeller, Marilyn Monroe, John and Jacqueline Kennedy, Alan Jay Lerner, Julius LaRosa, Yul Brynner, Marlene Dietrich, Anthony Quinn, Tennessee Williams.

Doctors are generally considered to be awesome figures: they seem to know things beyond the ken of ordinary mortals. Few people ever stop to think they are simply people themselves, often people with very big flaws. Even celebrities are not immune from this awe. Like everyone else, when they are in discomfort, they will put their complete trust in a man with a medical degree.

This was especially true in the 1950s—a time when it seemed that medical science could cure anything—instantly and painlessly. Penicillin was still a new drug, and there were all sorts of antibiotics following it onto the market. Dr. Jonas Salk had come up with a vaccine that would rid the world of polio. And there was a new term sweeping the nation—tranquilizers. Appropriately, the first of these—Miltown—was developed at the beginning of the decade, in 1950. Reserpine followed in 1952, and chlorpromazine in 1954. These drugs were working miracles against mental illness.

Because of the 1950s, America would become the most medicated society in the world. At the slightest discomfort, people went to their doctors, and invariably their doctors prescribed something. Unfortunately, the doctors did not yet know the full effects of what they were prescribing.

The children of the 1970s, enamored of their own drugs, would one day point to their parents' medicine cabinets and say, "See, I'm no different from you." Indeed, that would be true, but it would be no real justification for either generation. "Monkey see, monkey do," is a rather inadequate substitute for a moral creed. Just as inadequate as, "My doctor says . . ."

Dr. Max Jacobson was born in Germany in 1900. He had received his medical degree from the Frederick Wilhelm University of Berlin in 1925. Up until 1932, he had practiced medicine in Germany while doing research at the University of Berlin's Surgical Clinic on the possibility of transplanting tissues and organs. After the rise of Adolf Hitler and of anti-Semitism in Germany, Dr. Jacobson, who was a Jew, escaped to Czechoslovakia. In Prague, he received a patent for a sterilization process he had developed. In 1933, he immigrated to France, where he became an associate of the Pasteur Institute.

Keeping ahead of the Nazis step by step, he moved on to the United States in 1936, settling in New York and establishing a general practice, while continuing to distinguish himself through research—first as an assistant visiting surgeon at the New York City Cancer Institute, later through his own private research in vitamins, vitamin therapy, and amino acids.

It was a curious choice for a man who had witnessed the evils of a would-be "super race" in Germany, but Dr. Jacobson turned his efforts toward counteracting what he termed "the severe physical and emotional stresses of those who live and work in environments of continual high pressure." He seemed to enjoy having his office and reception room filled with high government officials, heads of state, business and industrial leaders, and the big names of the performing arts. He was certainly very proud of the fact he had once had an audience with Pope Pius XII and had once given advice to Winston Churchill's physician.

How could actors and singers, who are generally as insecure as ordinary people, not be impressed by such a man?

He told most of his patients what he was giving them in their injections was a vitamin mixture. When any of them asked for specifics, he smiled and told them, "None of your business." Because the injections seemed to work, very few of his patients asked again. However, they did find they had to go to see him for injections more and more frequently in order to keep feeling good.

Vitamins did play a part in Dr. Jacobson's mixture, but they formed only fifteen percent of the total; the rest was amphetamines, today known as speed.

Dr. Jacobson may or may not have known what he was doing to his celebrated patients in the beginning. It is safe to say, though, that he quickly learned the effects. Some of his patients went bankrupt paying for his treatments, a few going to work for him to keep getting the necessary injections. Some committed suicide. Some wisely broke away from him and survived well. Some survived as little more than vegetables.

Dr. Jacobson insisted he looked upon his patients as more than simply patients. He claimed they were his friends as well. He spent many social hours in the company of his famous patients, and it may have been that he gloried in the limelight. It may also have been that he grew to enjoy the great power he held over them. Eventually he would wield enormous power, for he would be supplying his treatment to the President of the United States at a most critical time in world affairs.

Eventually, Dr. Jacobson's power was checked; but in the twenty-five years while he was at his height, his treatments had drastic effects on the lives and careers of some of America's most talented and productive people.

Among them—Eddie Fisher.

Eddie recalls his early visits to Dr. Jacobson: "He gave me a shot and the voice came back. I was hooked from then on. The shots were comprised of vitamins as well as a form of drug. I never asked the name. The results were all I cared about."

In the weeks and months that followed his first visit to Jacobson, Eddie seemed able to accomplish more than ever. He was able to keep going long after ordinary people grew tired or slowed down. And when he did slow down, all Eddie had to do was to go back to Dr. Jacobson. Milton Blackstone, seeing the effects on Eddie, decided he would start taking the injections as well. With both their energies going full speed, nothing could hold them down. Eddie Fisher seemed to be everywhere at once.

Within a few short years, however, the drugs began to take their toll, both physically and emotionally. Later, when he tried to break away from the drugs to get his career moving again, he admitted, "I could not live without the shots. Most of that time is a blur to me." Like most people who become addicted to drugs, he began to live so totally within himself he could not even see his career and his following and his voice leaving him. In a sense, Eddie Fisher grew up to be a little boy. As such, he was the perfect idol for the 1950s, that decade when America truly began to want to return to childhood, giving up responsibility to father figures in government, medicine, and society in general.

The many faces of Eddie Fisher.

2. The Kid From South Philadelphia

The epitome of the 1950s was born in 1928 in South Philadelphia, just before the Crash. He was born to a lower class Jewish couple, Joseph and Kate Fisher. At birth, his prospects were not very good, even in America where—it was said—anyone could achieve anything. Even in the 1920s, when all the stops had been pulled out, anything was legal, including what was illegal.

South Philadelphia in the 1920s and 1930s was a lower class suburb, consisting mostly of immigrant families—Irish, Poles, Italians, and Jews. Located only four miles from downtown Philadelphia, it was a distinct and separate subculture. The houses were almost all wood-frame, and they usually had no more than three or four rooms. A family was lucky if it had a full bathroom, and a family the size of the Fishers often had to double up on beds.

The Irish, Poles, and Italians who lived in South Philadelphia were blue-collar laborers, most of them working in the factories that surrounded the area. The Jews, who comprised almost half the population of South Phillie, were mostly tradesmen, some selling out of shops, others moving their merchandise on racks, carts, or trucks on the streets.

At the time his fourth child was born, Joseph Fisher had a grocery store, but when the bottom fell out of the American economy in 1929, he lost the store and had to do his best as a street peddler. And his best would not prove to be very good. Willful and temperamental, he seemed incapable of handling money in such a way as to make it grow. Often unable to pay the rent, he led his family on a nomadic life, moving from house to house to keep ahead of the landlords.

Joseph was a short thin man who very rarely smiled. And when he did smile, it came out more as a leer than as a pleasant or happy expression. His small, dark, watchful eyes, his sharp beak-nose, and his large ears accentuated his always severe and disapproving expression. When he spoke to his wife or to his children, it was generally with a loud bark, and it was often in anger. He was not the sort of father his children could feel close to.

Fisher's wife Katherine, or Kate, however, was pretty, warm, motherly, and efficient, managing the continually growing Fisher family on little more than nothing. She was short and plump, with dark hair and eyes, and a brilliant, flashing smile. She was much more sensitive than her husband, attempting to shelter her children from his wrath, while enduring his abuses herself. She endured them because her religion and tradition told her that a woman must "obey," and because she felt a responsibility toward her children.

After all of her children were grown, Kate would divorce Joseph Fisher and remarry.

The relationship of Joseph and Kate Fisher was not an unusual one among Jewish-American families. Traditions remained strong for generations, and traditions placed great emphasis upon the male while denying all to the female. It did not matter whether the male was deserving of respect; it had to be given. At meals, the husband and father always received the largest or best portion; the oldest son received the next, and on down according to age. The daughters and wife would have whatever was left.

This system was not particularly damaging in families where the husband and father was naturally strong and sensitive and caring. But, in families where the husband and father was weak and insensitive, what should have been strength and love became selfishness, loudness, and hostility. The wife and mother, however, always accepted and endured. Very likely she had never received much love and attention when she was a child, and so she had an abundance of love stored up to shower on her children to make up for the inadequacy of their father.

Many jokes are made about Jewish mothers; not all of them are deserved. Jewish mothers were generally more capable than Jewish fathers; and, if they leaned a bit heavily on their devotion to their children, it was generally to make up for a lack of love and devotion and guidance from their husbands.

This kind of family relationship usually proves to present problems for the young Jewish boy, especially at adolescence. When he is thirteen, the boy enters synagogue where he is told that he is a man and must behave like a man. However, nowhere else in American society is he treated like a man at thirteen. If he has an inadequate father-figure to pattern himself after, he is doubly troubled. He is usually taught to disdain manual labor and strive toward studies and pursuits of the mind; if a boy is not particularly intelligent or studious, his troubles are further compounded. The result can be an arrogant, obnoxious, intemperate, self-indulgent, and insecure personality.

Joseph and Kate Fisher had been married in 1918. Kate was only sixteen at the time, and she hardly knew what to expect from marriage. Their first son, Sidney, was born in 1919. A daughter, Annette, was born brain-damaged in 1923; and another daughter, Miriam, was born in 1926.

In 1928, Kate was expecting the Fishers' fourth child. There were, as always, financial worries, but business in the United States was booming, and it seemed there was nowhere to go but up. It was a presidential election year, and Republicans were promising "a chicken in every pot, a car in every garage." On election day in November, voters endorsed that promise by electing Republican Herbert Hoover to the presidency.

Joseph Fisher's grocery store was a small one, but he had great hopes for expansion. If the country kept going the way it was going, he could support as big a family as he might want. Men with no more ability or resources than he had were making money hand over fist, often overnight. Prospects in this land of opportunity were limitless. Progress was visible everywhere—automobiles, telephones, airplanes, radios; the movies had sound now, and a man named George Eastman was promising that color would be next. Things were happening almost daily in 1928 to promise

Americans that the future looked rosier than it ever had before.

The least auspicious month of 1928 was August. A late summer torpor had set in after the political conventions. The presidential race between Herbert Hoover and Al Smith was getting off to a slow and uncertain start. That seemed to affect the economy; the stock market was sluggish, filled with cross-currents and irregularities, not clearly up or down.

On Friday, August 10, 1928, South Philadelphia was hot, humid, and overcast, promising—but not delivering—the relief of rain. It was not a particularly good day for Kate Fisher to go to the hospital to give birth to her fourth child. Joe and Kate had a boy and two girls already; they hoped the fourth would be another boy. They arrived at the hospital a little past midnight. While they waited to see the doctor, someone told them that there had been eleven babies born in the hospital the previous day, and that all of them had been girls. That piece of information did not lift the Fishers' spirits.

When Joseph and Kate finally were able to see the doctor, it was obvious that he was tired and much in need of sleep. But he was not beyond giving Kate a bright and hopeful smile, commenting, "I understand that you and your husband would like to have a boy this time."

Both parents nodded.

"Well," the doctor betrayed his weariness, "I'll tell you what I'm going to do. If you will have this baby of yours before eight o'clock tomorrow morning, so I can get home and have some breakfast and some rest, then I'll guarantee you a boy."

As the hours went by, it seemed that Kate Fisher was not going to be able to live up to her end of the bargain. The labor pains kept coming right on schedule, but the hours passed without their reaching the intensity that would suggest she was ready to deliver. By 7:30 in the morning, Joseph Fisher felt sure his wife could not give birth before 8:00.

But, at 7:45 A.M., Kate did deliver—and it was a boy.

If the Fishers had believed in astrology, they might have prayed that their child could be born a bit earlier or a bit later. But, being born at 7:45 A.M., their child had Virgo rising above the horizon, and people with Virgo rising—astrologers say—invariably have difficulty with partners, both marital and business. To make matters worse, the Sun, Mercury, Neptune, and Venus were all in Leo in his twelfth house of "Self-Undoing." Saturn was retrograde in Sagittarius, his fourth house, depriving him of the love and companionship of a good father.

The parents named the child Edwin Jack Fisher. But the nurses in the hospital gave him another name. With his black hair and his big brown eyes, he was a beautiful baby, and he became a favorite with them. They called him "Sonny Boy," after the currently popular Al Jolson song. When they held him or when they carried him in to his mother, they sang the song to him.

The surprising thing was that the nickname stuck, eventually getting shortened to "Sonny." And the crooning sounds seemed to have an effect upon the infant as well. From the time Sonny Fisher could talk, he sang. His mother often sang the old Jewish folksongs to her children, and the toddling Sonny quickly picked them up, repeating them word for word and note for note. Some said that Sonny Fisher was headed for a singing career from the very beginning.

The sentimental songs he heard as a child, combined with the Jolson nickname, no doubt influenced the direction his own musical style and manner took. After America sank into the depression of the 1930s, sentiment became something to hang onto. Even though they were poor, most families still had their radios, and they enjoyed listening to the happy crooning melodies of Jolson and Cantor and Crosby. The movies were still a cheap entertainment, and it was well worth the dime to escape into the glittering world of people who sang when they felt happy and always came out on top in the end. It gave them hope.

Joseph Fisher didn't have a great deal of hope in the early years of the depression. He had lost his grocery and was trying to make a living selling vegetables on the street. But it gave his pride and dignity a great deal of hurt and pain, and he inevitably took that hurt out on his family. Kate bore the brunt of his rage; she also had to bear the weight of caring for four children (one of whom needed constant attention), while a fifth was on its way. Sid, the oldest, was in school, and he occasionally helped his father sell vegetables. Miriam and Eddie were both good children; Annette was the difficult one. Miriam could help to look after Annette. As Kate grew heavier with child, she decided that Eddie would have to go and stay with her mother for awhile.

The one greatest influence on little Sonny Fisher in those early years turned out to be his maternal Grandmother. She adored him, showered him with attention, and praised him to the skies. When he was three, she predicted, "This one is going to be something special." And because she said it, little Sonny felt special.

His Grandmama would hold little Sonny on her lap, rocking him and singing to him. Once, when she was doing this, she thought the child had fallen asleep, so she stopped. Suddenly, he opened his big brown eyes, looked up at her, and sang back what she had just sung to him.

"The whole song he sang, Katherine!" she told her daughter proudly. "Like a Cantor he sings—only better!"

With singing, little Sonny received attention and praise. He liked that; singing made him feel special. Although he had won his first singing prize by age five—for singing best and loudest at a valentine party—his great ambition in early childhood was to sing with his sister Miriam in the choir at temple. When the choir director heard of Eddie's ambition, he invited the young boy to sing with them on Friday night. Young Sonny Fisher made his first public appearance, decked out in a white suit and black patent leather shoes. His face radiated with joy the whole evening.

However, Eddie was not always so eager to sing. Invariably, when company came to visit, his parents would ask Eddie to sing for the guests. At times, he would grow tired of this ritual and refuse. His child's intuition told him that all grown-ups did not listen appreciatively; some listened mockingly and teased him afterward because he was a child. On those occasions, he would be sent directly to bed as punishment.

The earliest years that Eddie can remember were the years of the deepest part of the Depression. The hopes of the nation for a chicken in every pot and a car in every garage were ridiculous even to consider by 1932; and whatever hopes and dreams Joseph and

Kate Fisher might have had at the time of Eddie's birth were long forgotten in the struggle for simple existence.

Amidst the bank closings and the loss of jobs and businesses, the American voters rejected the false hope of Hoover and the Republicans and elected Franklin Roosevelt to lead the nation out of its despair. The words, "The only thing we have to fear is fear itself," became a motto for a whole generation attempting pragmatically to build a better life. Positive attitudes, hope, and earnest striving were instilled into the consciousnesses of the children of the 1930s. That and the sense of people sharing and working together without false pride.

Eddie Fisher vividly remembers those difficult years as a period when his parents had to move from place to place because they couldn't pay their rent. The family never knew real starvation, but food was something his parents had to struggle to obtain for themselves and for their children. This seemingly never-ending struggle for survival caused Joseph Fisher to grow increasingly irascible. Thinking about his father in those early years, Eddie recalls, "He used to beat the heck out of me."

Eddie learned early to listen to his father, to watch him, and to be wary of him. He received very little, if any, affection from him, and the only affirmation he had was that if he was neither yelled at nor beaten, he must be okay. But, because Eddie also saw this oppression directed against his brothers and sisters as well as against him, he developed a caring and a compassion toward others. He was able to realize that his father's hostility was not directed against him personally.

Despite the family's poor economic situation, the Fisher family continued to grow. Eddie's sister Janet was born in 1932; and his brother Alvin appeared two years later. The last of the Fisher children would be born in 1939, when Eddie was eleven years old. With a family of that size, each of the children had to help out as he grew old enough to work. When he was old enough, Eddie had to help his father to sell fruits and vegetables.

Joseph Fisher had managed by this time to purchase a used auto which he had converted into a kind of truck he used to transport the fruits and vegetables from place to place. Eddie would meet him at various points around town, replenish his load of vegetables, and then go trudging off through the streets and alleys of Philadelphia, singing out, "Tomatoes, nice ripe tomatoes!"

For a time, Joseph Fisher was completely unable to work, so the family had to go on to the municipal relief roll. Even though a great many families all over the country were going through the same experience, it was humiliating for Eddie. He recalls, "I'd go down to the railway station where they handed out flour and vegetables. I'd hide the food under my coat so nobody would see it. The relief agency used to give out clothes, but I didn't like to wear the striped shirts; I thought everybody would know they came from the relief."

One thing that young Fisher had that few others had was a good voice, a talent for singing, and a desire to sing, and that was there from the very beginning. As shy and as insecure as he might be in other areas, singing was the one thing he knew he could do and do well. He also had ambition. He was not afraid of hard work, although he was determined not to have to spend the rest of his life selling vegetables on the streets of South Philadelphia. Through the movies, he had seen that life could be different from the way he and his family lived, and his ambition was to live with that kind of romance and affluence and style.

He had already determined these things when he was very young; but, in the earliest years, he confided in no one. He was afraid to confide these things because he had no idea of how he was going to achieve them. It might have helped if he had had a father he could have confided in; but it also might not have. A good father—in those circumstances—would certainly have pointed out how impractical a dream it was to become a singer.

He did confide his dream to one person—someone very far away, someone he knew but who didn't know him. Al Jolson had been responsible for his nickname. Eddie idolized Jolson, and he often spent hours by himself in his room just listening to Jolson's records. He wrote to Jolson asking for advice on how to become a star, how to plan his singing career. He didn't get a reply.

As the 1930s began to grow older, things began to improve for America, and they improved for the Joseph Fisher family as well.

However, Joseph Fisher's dream was gone. The Great Depression lasted a full ten years, and Joseph was no longer a young man. Now, considerably older and considerably more bitter, he would only be able to provide for his family, nothing more.

Eddie was twelve years old when the new decade began, and everything began to look much brighter to him. He wasn't as much a loner as he had been. He now had a couple of friends—good friends. Joey Forman, Bernie Rich, and Sonny Fisher were inseparable. Later they referred to themselves as the "Three Musketeers"—one for all, and all for one. But then they were referred to as "The Terrible Trio."

All three were South Philadelphia boys with similar family backgrounds and environment, and they had similar goals and interests, but they were not all alike. Bernie recalls that their friendship was deep and lasting "mainly because our personalities were all so different. Eddie was the shy serious one; Joey was always good for a laugh. Me, I was somewhere in between, always trying to shake off the name 'Coughdrop,' and make like a heavy."

Joey remembers Eddie as being intense and determined. "Talk about being serious, that was Eddie's second name. I'll never forget the first time we met, it was on a bus. He looked so lonely and serious that I wanted to crack a joke to see if I could make him smile. He was such a little kid, my first instinct was a protective one. After I talked to him, I discovered he wasn't the kind of guy who really needed mothering."

Eddie did confide his dreams to these two friends, and he was excited and encouraged that they had similar dreams. Joey wanted to be a comedian, and Coughdrop wanted to be a serious actor. Together, the three of them covered the entertainment spectrum.

Their first idea was to try to put on plays together, but they were hampered by the fact that they all went to different schools. Finally, they determined that they would put together an act and try to break into one of the talent contests that were constantly being held. They would meet at one of their homes after school and work on the act. These afternoons eventually stretched to evenings and to weekends as well.

"The Terrible Trio" was not much to look at. Joey was tall,

fairly attractive, and well developed, but he was the comic. Eddie and Bernie were short and skinny with too much hair. When they decided they were ready, they auditioned for Skipper Dawes' radio show on station WFIL, and they got the job, appearing with "The Magic Lady." They did songs, snappy patter, and commercials. In the beginning, they were each paid fifteen cents for carfare. Eddie walked the three miles to and from the radio station to save his fifteen cents.

To get their start, the boys would have worked for nothing; but when they saw that their act was catching on with the Skipper Dawes audience, they demanded a raise and got it—a big five dollars a week each. In less than two years, this went to fifteen dollars a week as they did four different radio programs regularly. The group was becoming quite popular locally, and Eddie especially with the teen-age girls.

It wasn't that Eddie was being precocious and chasing girls. On the contrary, he didn't even have a single girl friend. Joey explains, "We didn't really have much time for them. Once in awhile we would throw a party for them. Most of the time, Eddie was so timid and shy, he'd usually bring his sister. The girls didn't leave him alone for long though. Soon the invitations were filling his mailbox. Presto, chango, Eddie became the life of the party. He even took ten dancing lessons, and learned to dance."

One of the shows they were doing was sponsored by the Pet Milk Company. To advertise the show and their product, Pet Milk placed posters on the fronts of all the trolley cars in Philadelphia. Eddie's picture was on the ad, and on the picture lipstick began to appear.

This occurred after their salaries had been raised to fifteen dollars a week. Joey approached Eddie, "Your picture is all over the trolley cars; right?"

"Right," Eddie agreed.

"It's got lipstick all over it," Joey pursued, "right?"

"Right," Eddie acknowledged.

"So," Joey concluded, "you're popular; you should get more money."

But Eddie remained loyal to his friend. "That's not fair; you should get as much as me."

Together, they marched into the manager's office and demanded more money. They got it—eighteen dollars a week each, a phenomenal salary for fifteen-year-olds in those days. After that, the boys shook hands and made a pact; they promised that, if one made it big in show business, he should help the other two. The unusual thing was not that they made the pact, but that they remembered it. When Eddie finally made the big step, he remembered his promise to Joey and Bernie.

These were the early 1940s, the war years. For many, it was a frightening and troubling time. For most people, there was prosperity, but there were other kinds of hardship. There were shortages of various kinds, and there was rationing. And boys a few years older than Eddie were marching off to fight in Europe and the Pacific.

The changes that took place on the homefront were drastic ones; all of them were described by business, labor, and the government as temporary changes for the duration of the emergency. Some of them, however, became permanent changes. But these—after the war was over—went unnoticed by the average person. Business and government grew bigger, and worked hand-in-hand with labor. Advertising burgeoned into a major industry. As always, during a war, science and technology took a great leap forward. After the war was over, America would have a vast number of new products—everything from spray cans to jet planes and nuclear energy.

However, there were other changes taking place that were even more important to Sonny Fisher—changes in styles, especially in music. Swing was in, and the Big Band sound was making room for individual singing stars. One in particular attracted thirteen-year-old Fisher. His name was Frank Sinatra; he was a skinny little kid from Hoboken, New Jersey, and the girls were literally swooning for him.

When Sinatra gave a concert at Convention Hall in Philadelphia in 1941, Eddie attended. He sat clinging to the edge of his seat, mesmerized by the performance. He was aware of how Sinatra's charisma and vocal talent crept over the audience and held it. *That,* Sonny Fisher realized, was what he had to strive to achieve with his singing.

Immediately, he realized there was some similarity between them. They were both small and skinny; they were both from minority backgrounds and from lower-class areas of big cities. Most important, there was a similarity between their voices and the way they crooned their songs.

Frank Sinatra became his new idol, and the records he played alone in his room were Sinatra records.

He tried to learn how Sinatra had gotten his breaks, hoping to figure out how he could get his own career going. Sinatra had begun with radio and Eddie had already taken that step. Sinatra had followed up by landing a job with a Big Band. But Eddie had no idea how he could accomplish this second step.

It was 1945; Eddie had just turned seventeen. He was in the eleventh grade at Simon Gratz High School. He was appearing regularly on "The Magic Lady Supper Club," a Philadelphia radio show sponsored by the Lit Brothers department store. He had managed to earn himself a piano to practice on by singing with a temple choir. He had done everything he could do while living at home in Philadelphia. Somehow he had to get away and make his next break.

Luck was in his corner: Skipper Dawes made the next move for him. Skipper approached him one day, looking very pleased with himself, offering, "Eddie, I think you are ready to try your voice out on a larger audience and in public."

Eddie's heart leaped; his mind raced. What?

"Buddy Morrow's band is coming to town. They are in need of a singer, and I have arranged for you to audition for him." Skipper proceeded to give his young protege some advice. "Look, whether or not you get the job is going to depend on how much confidence you have in yourself. If you don't have any confidence in you, no one else is going to have any either."

It was a very scared seventeen-year-old who auditioned for Buddy Morrow, but it was also a very hopeful young man, and Eddie did his best. He was hired for the job on the spot. Knowing that he would be an overnight sensation, he promptly changed his name to Sonny Edwards. In the 1940s Jewish entertainers were still self-conscious about being Jewish, and there was still considerable anti-Semitism around, especially among the powerful Jews in the New York entertainment world.

Sonny Edwards was headed toward New York as a singer with the Buddy Morrow band. He knew that nothing but success, praise, and excitement would follow—just the way it always happened in the movies.

Top: The two Eddies with Jennie Grossinger. Bottom: The two Eddies sing a duet.

Eddie's proud parents.

Teenage friends with Skipper Dawes and Eddie Cantor.

Bernie, Eddie, Skipper and Joey.

3. Sonny Edwards Goes To Town

New York in the 1940s was at its peak of glamor, sophistication, and excitement. Its population had reached seven and one-half million. There was a housing shortage, and people were having to double up in apartments—if they could even find one. The theater world was bustling with excitement over a new kind of musical, *Oklahoma.* Nightclubs and restaurants were doing a booming business; it seemed the whole population of seven and a half million wanted to go out and dance until dawn. And they were dancing to sweet and sentimental songs like "It Might As Well Be Spring," "It's A Grand Night for Singing," and "Laura."

It seemed to be just the right place and the right time for young Sonny Edwards to be.

But singing with a band was not at all what he had expected. The bands had their own styles and their own sounds, and—whoever their singer happened to be at the time—their singer had to conform to that style. There was no room for individuality; a song had to be sung the way it always had been from the very beginning; the singer had to sound like the singer who had made it popular. This was something that Eddie had not anticipated.

His job with Buddy Morrow lasted only a few weeks.

His mother pressured him to come home and finish high school, but Eddie was obstinate. He was determined to remain in New York and to find another job singing. Returning to South Philadelphia would be acknowledging defeat; he might never get another opportunity there. His parents sent him money, and his friends Joey and Bernie joined him, moving in with him to share expenses.

Having Joey and Bernie with him lifted Eddie's spirits. Together, they faced the cold impersonality of New York with the wild and unrestrained exuberance of youth. They had no idea of the impossibly difficult obstacles they faced; anything was possible to them because they were special—they had talent.

Like most seventeen-year-olds, they did occasionally have their differences and disagreements, but they generally didn't last long. Eddie admits rather nostalgically, "We had our squabbles, but no one played arbitrator. If Joey and Bernie had a battle, I'd let them settle their own differences. When I had an argument with either of them, the third party likewise kept out of it."

However, both Joey and Bernie agree that, back then, Eddie was the most disturbed over their minor conflicts. But, after all, Eddie was the most sensitive of the three. Bernie remembers, "Sometimes, when Eddie thought he'd hurt either of us, you could almost see the lump in his throat."

In New York, there was very little time for squabbles. There was too much to do and see. The three of them scavenged everywhere to learn about job openings and auditions. Occasionally, Eddie did get a brief job, but nothing really good until a spot with Charlie Ventura's band came along. It wasn't exactly the kind of work he wanted—he was singing out in the suburbs, again having to mimic other band singers—but at least it was work, and it lasted a few weeks.

When it was over, he was back on the streets looking for work again, and having to call home for money. He was practically broke when he happened to be in a coffee shop and overheard a waiter talking about auditions being held at the Copa, New York's top nightclub. This—Eddie was certain—had to be his big break. It was the "In" place for singers to get started; anybody who appeared there was seen and heard by all the big names in the business. If he had talent, everybody who was anybody would hear about it instantly.

He had to plan his approach carefully. Facing himself squarely and honestly, he knew he had to have advice and help. He decided to call his mentor, Skipper Dawes, in Philadelphia, to ask for his advice. Skipper immediately realized how important this audition could be for his protege, and he decided to come to New York to help him.

Skipper knew that they had to see the Copacabana owner, Monte Proser. The Copa was (and is) situated on 60th Street between Madison and 5th Avenues. During the day, without its glamorous guests, it looked cold, dark, and barren. They had some difficulty finding the famed nightclub owner, but finally located him in the dark shadows of the Copa basement. In the darkness, Proser seemed to be a stern and enigmatic man.

"If you wanna audition," he barked out gruffly, "there's a piano over there."

It was not at all the kind of scene Eddie and his mentor had envisioned. Eddie was a bit scared because he could not see the reaction of his audience; and Skipper was uncomfortable because he could barely see the music to accompany Eddie on the piano.

However, the young singer mustered his courage and proceeded to sing six songs, one a special number that Skipper had arranged for him. When the audition was over, Proser grunted encouragingly, "Sounds all right. Better come upstairs so I can see what you look like."

With his hopes clutching at his throat, Eddie followed Skipper and the Copa owner upstairs. There, in the bright lights, Proser howled with laughter.

"Why, you're only a little kid," he exclaimed. "I can't use babies around here."

Eddie's hopes were dashed; his heart sagged; but, thinking quickly, he grasped at a straw. "I'll be eighteen in August."

Proser eyed the young singer suspiciously, with a glint of humor in his eyes.

"Eighteen," Eddie persisted, resisting the impulse to add, "scout's honor."

After lengthy consideration, Proser gave in. "Okay, come back in October. I'll be starting my fall shows; I'll give you a job then."

That was not the answer that Eddie had wanted to hear, but it was better than an outright "no." Once Proser's resistance was broken, Skipper Dawes knew that this was the moment his protege had to get as much as he possibly could from the influential nightclub owner. He took the moment to discuss as fully as possible Eddie's future as a singer. Being frank himself, he asked for frankness from Proser.

They were all agreed upon one thing—the seventeen-year-old singer did have a good voice. At the moment, he had little else; he still looked like a skinny, shy, goofy kid. He lacked experience; he lacked exposure. In time, he might possibly be a headliner; but right now, he just wasn't ready for the Copa audience.

When he had the time, or when he was pressed to take the time, Monte Proser had about as big a heart as it was possible to have in show business. Now that he was pressed to take the time with Eddie Fisher, he realized that he could help the kid.

He got on the telephone and made a phone call that set up the most important connection in Eddie's career. He called a man named Milton Blackstone.

Eddie anxiously paced the floor while Proser talked long distance to Milton, who was at Grossinger's, a resort in upstate New York.

"Milt," Proser began, "I got a boy here I think you should meet. He's got a good voice, but he's just a kid. I think he needs some on-the-job training."

The anxiety of waiting for the silence to end, to know the response from Blackstone, was almost unendurable. It seemed like an eternity before Proser said, "Good. I'll send him up to see you. You'll know him right off; he's a skinny kid with a lot of curly hair."

Eddie was aware vaguely that Grossinger's was a Jewish resort in the Catskill Mountains, but he had absolutely no idea who Milton Blackstone was or what he could do for him. He knew only that if Monte Proser thought he could help him, Milton Blackstone must be somebody important. That, he certainly was, despite the fact that few people in the general public knew his name.

The man who would eventually be responsible for the success of Eddie Fisher was born Milton Schwartzstein, in Jersey City, New

Jersey, in 1906. He was one of six children born to a mother who was a veritable bundle of energy. In addition to raising six very bright children, she ran a millinery shop, where she made the very fashionable Adrienne line of custom hats. As if that was not enough, she was involved in community affairs, being one of the founders of the Jewish Home and Hospital in Jersey City.

When Milton was in his freshman year at Lehigh University, he developed a serious infection in his jawbone. Not only did the infection require surgery, but it also restricted his activities. Mrs. Schwartzstein decided to send Milton to a small summer resort in the Catskill Mountains. It was a quiet, family-type establishment, and there was not much to tempt Milton into activity, since there wasn't much anyone could do there.

The meeting between Jennie Grossinger and Milton Schwartzstein was an auspicious one. Jennie had been responsible for turning what had been a seven-room farmhouse in 1914 into a hotel that was capable of housing five hundred guests by 1924. Jennie had a great influence on Milton, and Milton in turn had a great influence on Jennie and Harry's son, Paul. He was asked to stay on as a member of the family to tutor young Paul and learn more about the hotel business. Milton had a lot of ideas about how Grosssinger's could be enlarged, improved and promoted.

While setting about handling the promotion and public relations of the resort, he entered into what became a long, dedicated and mutual friendship with Jennie Grossinger. It was he who laid the format for her becoming the world's most famous hostess.

In 1930, at the age of twenty-four, Milton Schwartzstein left Grossinger's, Anglicized his name to Blackstone, and set up The Blackstone Agency on West 57th Street in New York to handle advertising, promotion, and publicity.

Its first client was Grossinger's.

Milton quickly learned the ins and outs of the Broadway scene, and his name and face became familiar to people in the entertainment business. His manner was suave, and his appearance was slick and sophisticated. He had a genial, appealing face, and his black, sleeked-down hair and his impeccable apparel marked him as a gentleman. Few men had a greater capacity for friendship;

people liked him instantly and responded well to his quick wit and vivacious personality. When he came up with the idea of offering entertainment at Grossinger's, he had no trouble convincing celebrities to try out their new acts at the resort.

He also attracted new talent—young people who were just getting started—among them opera singers Robert Merrill and Jan Peerce, comedians Sam Levenson and Red Buttons, and singer-comedienne Betty Garrett.

Within a few years, the name Milton Blackstone became one to be reckoned with in entertainment circles. He was known and respected by the biggest producers and impresarios on Broadway, many of whom became his clients: Billy Rose, Mike Todd, Carl Erbe, Monte Proser, and Bob Weitman of the Paramount. And all of these men got to know and respect Grossinger's.

In 1934, when Milton arranged for middleweight champion Barney Ross to train at Grossinger's for his fight against Jimmy McLarnin, Grossinger's became famous all over the world. The place was packed with publicity people, newspaper writers and photographers. As a result of all of Milton's efforts, Grossinger's continued to grow and eventually became the most important resort in the area, possibly the most important on the entire east coast, and Jennie Grossinger became known as one of the finest hostesses in the nation.

Milton's promotion work was halted during World War II, so that he could contribute to the war effort by assisting his brother Leo in his shipbuilding industry. But, by 1946, he was back with The Blackstone Company, and back lending his efforts toward the greater success of Grossinger's.

On that summer's day in 1946 when Milton Blackstone first laid eyes on Eddie Fisher, he wondered if Monte Proser were playing some kind of joke on him. Proser was a good friend: he had suggested the idea of having Barney Ross train at Grossinger's. Proser had also been telling him that what would really put the resort on the map was to have a major talent "discovered" there. But there was no way this skinny kid with pimples and a mop of curly hair could be a major talent.

And the problem that Monte Proser had—the fact that Eddie Fisher was under-age and could not legally perform in a nightclub—was just as much a problem for Grossinger's as it was for the Copacabana. There was no way, Milton determined instantly, that he could assume the responsibility for this young fellow in a nightclub atmosphere. In fact, a resort like Grossinger's was even more risky for a seventeen-year-old than a nightclub: after dark, some women who came to places like this grab hold of anything in pants without bothering to think about age.

Eddie pleaded with Milton, explaining that he was broke. Everybody was saying that he wasn't ready; well, he had to live and get experience somehow until he was ready.

This, Milton finally realized, was the point Monte Proser had been trying to make by sending the young singer to him: stars are not born overnight; they have to be developed and nurtured so that, when they are ready, they can spring forth as overnight sensations. What better place than a resort like Grossinger's?

But a seventeen-year-old kid with pimples?

Finally, Milton gave in: Eddie could work at the hotel for the summer—but he could not perform in the nightclub until *after* his eighteenth birthday. In the meantime he could do various jobs around the place—wait tables, work as a boatboy handing out oars to the guests, caddy. And he could sit and watch the professionals rehearse their act. He would start at $20 a week; and, when he started singing, that would be raised to $50.

If Milton Blackstone were not overly impressed with young Eddie Fisher, neither was Eddie overwhelmed by the great and powerful promoter. The man who had been known for his youthful suavity and charm was now forty, and he was beginning to acquire the appearance of a successful middle-aged businessman. His hair was graying and receding, and he was acquiring a paunch. It rankled Eddie that Milton treated him so much like a begger. But, Eddie realized, that was exactly what he had to be at this point. There was no way around it. He might easily be back in New York starving.

That was pretty much what Eddie's friend Joey was doing. But Eddie was about to change that. Milton had been determined to keep the under-aged Eddie away from the hotel atmosphere as much as possible, so he had set him up in a room in a secluded area near the spot where they were building the air landing strip for the resort. Surreptitiously, Eddie slipped Joey into his room and very quietly smuggled food in each day.

Gradually Milton and Eddie warmed up to each other, with Milton assuming the role of a father to the young boy, a very stern and a very protective father. Even after Eddie's birthday, when he was finally allowed to perform, he was allowed to sing only until midnight. "If you are in the middle of a song," Milton insisted, "when that clock strikes twelve, it's off the stage and off to bed for you."

Another stipulation Milton made was that Eddie had to open a bank account and save at least ten dollars out of every paycheck. When Eddie asked why, Milton explained, "So you won't have to take any job just to eat. You will have enough money to make a choice."

However, Milton could not keep the young man completely sheltered. Eddie was finally beginning to notice girls, and there was one in particular he had noticed, but she wouldn't pay any attention to him. Her name was Lenore Pesin, and she was a member of the Grossinger family. Tania Grossinger, who was just a child herself, recalls in her book, *Growing Up At Grossinger's* (McKay, 1975):

> He (Eddie) was not a very attractive kid, by any means. He was terribly underweight, hadn't yet been cured of his adolescent acne, and was very insecure with the girls. He had a crush on my cousin Lenore Pesin his first summer, I remember, and used to give me nickels if I could get Lenore to say hello to him. Fortunately, I didn't have to depend on him for pocket money.

If Eddie was unlucky in love, he was at least lucky in the excellent musical training he was receiving. Eddie had no real education in music. Whatever he knew he had learned mostly by ear—listening to the recordings of Jolson and Sinatra and others. He had picked up a little bit of information about musical notation from here and there, but not enough to be able to sight-read. Nor did he have a great sense of rhythm. Eddie himself admits that he danced "like an elephant." Eddie Ashman, the orchestra conductor recalls his early experiences with young Fisher: "He didn't know one note or key from another or even what a downbeat meant. I would have to tap him on the shoulder with my baton when it would be time for him to start singing!"

But Eddie got through his first Labor Day weekend at the resort, and he gloried in the experience. Now, surely, he was ready for the Copa. As soon as he got back to New York, he went to see Monte Proser to remind him of his job offer.

"I'll bet you thought you'd never see me again," Eddie announced.

Proser admitted that the hope had crossed his mind; but he had made a promise, and he would stick to it. Eddie was hired to start at the beginning of October. He would appear to sing and dance with the famous Copa showgirls and to warm up the stage for the headliners. On one occasion, however, Eddie recalls, "I had to stage my act after a lot of celebrities had performed because it was celebrity night. I was scared to death to come on stage."

Despite his fears, the young entertainer did get respectful attention, even from the celebrities. He met Perry Como, who came backstage and complimented him; and one night Frank Sinatra was in the audience. Obviously Sinatra recognized that Eddie was attempting to follow in his footsteps, because, when Eddie had finished, Sinatra winked and mocked a swoon, saying, "Ooooo, Eddie!"

This was the big time, and Eddie could see his dreams within grasp. Proudly, he invited his parents to come and see him, to prove to them that he could achieve what he had set out to achieve. But the results were disappointing. Eddie recalls, "My mother and father got in from Philadelphia to see me. I thought they would be very impressed with my act; but instead, when I saw them after the show, they couldn't talk about anything else except how they had actually sat at the table with Dick Powell and June Allyson."

Eddie correctly determined that this was the right time for him to get himself an agent. He was working; he could be seen and hired to appear elsewhere. He found one with no difficulty, a man of some reputation by the name of Cal Irving.

There is a very common misconception about agents, even among experienced talents who often unwisely assume that an agent is going to work for them, to try to get them more jobs. But this is not generally the case. The agents do work for their ten percent, but most of them cannot devote much time to the talents who are not already bringing in money. Big name talents bring in calls for jobs simply on the basis of their reputations; unknowns have to go out and pound the pavement looking for work. Once the job offers are in hand, the agent can negotiate terms and handle the money.

It is the rare agent who will go out and do the footwork, the job-seeking for his client. The agent that Eddie Fisher acquired was not one of the rare ones. When his appearance at the Copa ended at the end of October, Eddie found his career had come to a screeching halt. His appearance there had not been such a phenomenal success that his career took off and soared upward. Nor was it a failure, which made his career plummet downward. It was simply that his career went nowhere.

One good thing that came from the Copa engagement was a girl, Eddie Fisher's first love.

The Copacabana is noted for its beautiful chorus girls. At the time Eddie appeared, there were ten of them. Nine of them were older than Eddie, but the tenth was Eddie's age. The nine older girls set themselves up as matchmakers, to pair Eddie with eighteen-year-old Joan Wynn.

Eddie admits they didn't have to push him very hard. "Joan Wynn was the most beautiful girl I had ever seen," he explains. "For me, it was love at first sight. I fell in love with the prettiest girl in the Copa line. She was Irish as a Kilkenny kitten and twice as lovable."

Joan fell for Eddie just as hard as he did for her. There were plenty of men vying for her attention—rich, suave, handsome, any kind she could have wanted. But there was something about the shy, insecure young singer that attracted her. It may have been the fact that he seemed to need someone so much. It is more likely that she loved him despite that fact. Whatever it was, the romance continued for the next three years.

During those three years, the biggest problem for Eddie was that he was almost continually out of work. Occasionally, he would get a job, but usually it would be some cheap cabaret in an out-of-the-way spot, and it never led anywhere. In 1948, he managed to get a spot on the Arthur Godfrey Talent Scouts Program, and he won, but the appearance did him little good. It did lead to his being hired by the radio show, "Stop the Music." However, he didn't really consider what he was doing as performing. Generally he got only a few bars into a song before he had to stop.

Without work, Eddie quickly ran out of money. Without money, he had to resort to locating someone who would let him move in for awhile. Sometimes, he found himself sleeping on cold floors or in hard bathtubs. To keep himself alive, he ate chocolate bars. Even the best of friends couldn't put up with this sort of thing forever; and, invariably, Eddie would turn to Joan to lend him the money to keep going. For awhile, her family allowed him to stay at their home in Brooklyn.

Joan had to provide Eddie with other things beside money. She gave his morale a boost whenever he needed it, she gave him advice, and she offered him criticism. The longer she stayed in the relationship with Eddie, the more astonished Joan became at how deeply insecure he was. Eddie didn't know how to dress; Joan told him what clothes looked best on him. Eddie didn't like to go begging to producers for appointments; Joan got him appointments and auditions with producers. He couldn't even judge which were his best songs; and Joan had to give him advice on that.

But what troubled Joan most was Eddie's immaturity. She would explain to friends, "He can sing beautifully, but he's just so scared to death of a live audience and so lacking in self-confidence that he just dies on stage the minute his song is finished. I've got to nag him so he'll start growing up."

Unfortunately, nagging couldn't accomplish that. Nagging simply led to quarrels, and the quarrels only made Eddie more depressed. It was like quicksand: the more Joan tried to make Eddie stand on his own two feet, the more he slipped down. During one of the worst phases of this, Joan confided to friends, "When

Eddie isn't working, he acts as if the whole world is in conspiracy against him.''

If Eddie happened to spot someone they knew when they were out together, he would make Joan duck with him in and out of the back doors of restaurants or hide in doorways, just to avoid explaining to friends and acquaintances that he wasn't working. It did no good at all for her to try to convince Eddie that being out of work was nothing to be ashamed of.

Eventually, she began to realize she could not make Eddie grow up. As much as she loved him, she could not sustain this kind of one-sided relationship forever. From time-to-time, she would try to end the relationship, to break off with Eddie. But he would not stand for it. On one occasion, he even threatened to jump off a roof if Joan did not come back to him. She didn't want to risk finding out if he would really follow through with his threat, so she gave in.

Joan Wynn would not be the last woman to fall into this kind of a relationship with Eddie. Whether she was the first is debatable; after all, Eddie had had a mother, a grandmother, and four sisters, all of whom had doted upon him.

The relationship with Joan went on, with almost no change in the pattern, for almost three years. Early in 1949, however, Eddie did something to pull himself out of the pattern. He used his friendship with Milton Blackstone to get an appointment with Bob Weitman, manager of the Paramount Theater in New York. In what he had determined would be a last desperate attempt to get his career on course, he dropped his pride and went begging.

The Paramount was where Frank Sinatra had set records, and had had the bobbysoxers of the 1940s swooning in the aisles. Eddie explained to Weitman that he had always wanted to sing at the Paramount, and that he would be willing to work there for nothing.

Weitman recognized the desperation in Eddie's plea. He agreed to book Eddie, but Eddie would not be the main attraction. The pay would be $75 a week. The Paramount was a movie theater that offered live entertainment between shows. The live entertainment was often as much an attraction as the motion pictures. In the case of Frank Sinatra, it had proved to be the main attraction. During the intermission, Eddie would get to sing two numbers with organ accompaniment.

Outside, the movie got top billing: *"The Furies;* Barbara Stanwyck, Wendell Corey, Walter Huston." Below that was listed the live entertainment: "In Person; Mills Brothers; Al Berne; Eddie Fisher & the Bobby Byrne Orch."

After three years of going nowhere, Eddie had determined that this was the real test. If nothing happened to his career after playing the Paramount, he might as well give up.

And nothing did happen. After the engagement ended, he was simply out of work again, living on crackers, chocolate bars, and milk. He could not go back to bumming from Joan again; his depression sank so deep this time that he could not face even her.

So he went home to South Philadelphia, finally admitting defeat.

4. Creating Eddie Fisher

It had been almost four full years since Eddie had left Philadelphia for New York. His twenty-first birthday was rapidly approaching, and he finally had to take stock of himself. He left assuming all he had to do was get on a stage and sing, and he would be recognized for his talent. He learned that was not enough; he needed experience and exposure. He tried that, and learned it wasn't enough; his talent still went unrecognized. He now assumed there was nothing more he could do.

Kate Fisher recalls the moment when Eddie came home: "The only time I ever really saw my Sonny cry was when he had finished one of his New York jobs. He had decided to stay on there, waiting for offers to come in, but they never came. With no job, he had no money. He spent hours going from one producer's office to another. Then one Wednesday morning in late summer, my Sonny came back home to Philadelphia. He walked in the front door where I was working in my living room. He looked at me with distress written all over his face. 'Mama, Mama,' and I turned surprised, wondering what he was doing home at that particular time."

Mrs. Fisher handled the situation very well. She may have babied her son when he was a baby. But he was a man now, and she could tell this was a very serious matter to Eddie. She recognized the misery in her son's face, but she asked no questions, choosing to ignore his condition.

Eddie wandered around the living room, waiting for sympathy. Finally, he shook his head and walked over to the couch, burying his head in a pillow, and began to cry.

"So hard he cried that morning," Kate Fisher remembers.

After she could stand it no longer, she walked over to where he was sitting and cautiously touched him. "Eddie," she asked simply, "please tell me what is troubling you."

He blurted it out. "I'm licked, Mama. I can't go on. I'm all washed up as a singer."

She let him cry a bit longer, to get as many of the tears out of his system as possible, then she spoke with a slight trace of mockery in her voice; "Sonny, you remember when you were a little boy? How once you said to me, 'Mama, when I get big, I want to be a singer. And if I can't be a singer, then I might as well become a street cleaner?' "

Eddie looked at her and nodded.

"Well, Sonny," she smiled at him, "what are you planning to do after you finish crying? Are you going down to the board of sanitation and apply for a job?"

At that, Eddie had to laugh; and after that he couldn't go back to crying. He sat calmly and explained the whole situation to his mother. He talked about Milton Blackstone and Grossinger's; he talked about Monte Proser and the Copa; and he talked about Bob Weitman and the Paramount. Apparently, he told her, it all meant nothing. No matter what he did, his agent could not get him decent bookings. He still could not get the kind of recognition that meant success.

"Maybe you don't need this agent," Kate suggested. "Maybe you should call that nice man who got you the job at Grossinger's."

Eddie looked at her blankly, about to protest, "But . . ."

Kate Fisher handed her son the telephone. "Just tell him what you've been telling me."

Eddie refused, so Kate Fisher took the phone and dialed. When she finally located Milton Blackstone, he was puzzled at Eddie's despondency.

"Tell him not to give up just yet," he instructed Kate. "He has put too much into a singing career to quit now. Send him up to Grossinger's this weekend, and I'll see what I can do for him."

After much prodding from his mother, Eddie agreed to go to Grossinger's to see Milton.

While these events were taking place in the life of Eddie Fisher, tremendous changes were taking place in America and in the world. The previous year, to everyone's surprise and to the chagrin of many, the honest and forthright Harry Truman was elected president of the United States. But late in 1949, Truman and a number of other honest, forthright politicians were beginning to be needled by Senator Joseph McCarthy, who was accusing a vast number of political opponents of being "Communist sympathizers." The United States recognized the new state of Israel and the new state of Vietnam, and there were rumblings of a civil war beginning in Korea. With the opening of *Death of a Salesman* on Broadway, critics were heralding a great new playwright in Arthur Miller, a master of morbid introspection.

As the new medium of television grew, people speculated upon its effects. While the preponderance of popular music was still sentimental, there were some complaints at the amazing success of songs such as, "Riders in the Sky," "Mule Train," "Rag Mop," and "The Thing."

The 1940s were on their way out, and the 1950s were about to be unleashed, with changes so rapid—and oftentimes so subtle—that the American people would not fully realize their effects.

Late in the summer of 1949, Eddie Fisher and Milton Blackstone were sitting at Grossinger's planning just such a change. Certainly they had no idea of the wide impact their action would have upon the entertainment world. All they were going to do was to "create" a "new discovery" named Eddie Fisher. It never occurred to them that others would later follow their example.

The problem was that there had not been the kind of overwhelming response to Eddie Fisher that there had been to Frank Sinatra. Some people had suspected the Frank Sinatra craze had been staged. Of course, no one could hire massive crowds like that. But one could very easily stage an audience response in a nightclub. And if a major entertainment figure were on hand to witness this new sensation, to "discover" him, then the event would make news. The massive response should follow. Hollywood had been doing that sort of thing with movie stars for years. Why couldn't the music business?

Grossinger's big attraction for the Labor Day weekend was the illustrious Eddie Cantor. Grossinger's would also book Eddie Fisher. They would arrange for press and celebrities to be present.

Milton approached Eddie Cantor with the idea, suggesting to Cantor he might take Fisher on as his "discovery," asking him to join him on his tour. Cantor was astonished at the idea, and he refused.

But Milton Blackstone was not discouraged. He found out Cantor planned to rehearse at five o'clock. He arranged for Eddie Fisher to rehearse at 4:45. When Cantor came in at 5:00, he heard the young singer, and Milton was able to get him to go along with the plan. However, Cantor persisted, if the audience didn't respond on Labor Day as planned, he could still refuse.

Milton "papered" the audience that night with selected young people. Some were stationed down front, some at the back and sides. They were instructed to applaud wildly when Eddie Fisher was introduced and when he sang. Eddie was to do the warm-up just before Cantor came on.

Fisher appeared on schedule and sang, "I'm Sitting On Top of the World." The audience went wild.

Eddie Cantor came on, feigning amazement. He said, "Ladies and gentlemen, I've heard many a crooner in my day, but this boy isn't a crooner, he's a singer. This boy is going to be something. I haven't seen anything like it in twenty years."

Cantor looked at Eddie and spoke to him, "I am very serious. You are going to be something. You are going to make a living singing."

Fisher replied nervously, "I don't even know whether I'm getting paid here tonight."

"Did you eat tonight?" Cantor asked.

"Yes," Fisher admitted.

"Then," Cantor quipped, "You have been paid."

After the laughter died down, Cantor got serious. He explained to the audience that he was going to get off the stage now to let Eddie Fisher do an encore, adding, "If you agree with me about this boy, after he sings, please applaud, and I'll invite him on my cross-country tour."

Eddie did his encore, and the uproar from the audience was wild. He sang a second encore, and the walls seemed to shake. Cantor came back onstage, threw his arm around Fisher and announced, "September 13th I open in Lancaster, Pennsylvania, then Reading, and on to Chicago for ten days. You have a job!"

Eddie Fisher's face glowed.

Cantor quipped, "Don't look so happy 'till I tell you what I am going to give you." Then, he added, "I'll bring my two lawyers; you just bring Blackstone."

Labor Day at Grossingers in 1949 was only the beginning of the creation of "Eddie Fisher, Teen Idol." Although the next year was an exciting one for Eddie, it was not all roses. He still did not blossom into a star overnight.

Eddie did go on the tour with Eddie Cantor, and the audience response was good. He also joined Cantor for appearances on Cantor's television show, "The Colgate Comedy Hour." Because he was the protege of such an eminent entertainer as Cantor, he also had appearances with Milton Berle and George Jessel.

Together Cantor and Blackstone helped Fisher obtain a recording contract with RCA Victor. At the time, RCA had two labels: the Bluebird label for newcomers; the Black Label for their top stars. Of course, Fisher was signed to record on Bluebird; but after only three records, he joined their Black Label line.

His first record—"My Bolero" and "Foolish Tears"—was cut in October of 1949. When it came out it was immensely popular for a first recording. Immediately, Bluebird recorded another single—"Sorry" and "Yesterday's Roses"—before the year was out. His last Bluebird single—"Am I Wasting My Time on You" and "I Love You Because"—was cut early in 1950.

The last few months of 1949 were exciting ones for Eddie; he was feeling on top of the world. Now that he had regained his pride, his romance with Joan Wynn returned to a good footing. He invited her to Grossinger's for the Labor Day festivities, both to impress her and to show her off. And Eddie's friends at Grossinger's were impressed with his girl.

Paul Grossinger recalls sitting by the pool with a married couple as Joan passed by wearing a skimpy bathing suit. The wife turned to her husband and remarked, "Honey, if you ever cheat on me with a girl who looks like that, I'll forgive you."

Despite the success, money was still occasionally tight for Eddie, and for his friends Joey and Bernie—and so they all remained close and interdependent.

The 1950s were ushered in for Eddie Fisher at a very significant spot—Bill Miller's Riviera in New Jersey, the nightclub that had been such an important step in the career of Frank Sinatra.

When the invitation came from Bill Miller, it came as a bit of a disappointment to Eddie. It was for a private New Year's Eve party, not for a public engagement. He was reluctant to accept, hoping to hold out for something better for his first appearance at the famed spot. But Milton disagreed.

"Definitely say yes," Milton advised. "You can never tell what a little thing like that will lead to." Looking stern and fatherly, he asked, "How could you not want to do this?"

Eddie still did not seem to know how to play the games that would build a career in entertainment. His attitude appeared simplistic and egocentric. He seemed unable to understand that other people in show business had egos to be satisfied, and that they also had to think of money and income and other such mundane matters. Nobody gave anything away just because a kid had a nice voice. He had to earn his place among them.

On Milton's advice, and much against his own inclinations, Eddie Fisher made the appearance at Bill Miller's Riviera on New Year's Eve of 1949. When it was over, it did not seem to spell overwhelming success: no offer of an engagement was made immediately afterward, nor did one come for several months.

The first five months of 1950 were not as busy for Eddie as the last three months of 1949 had been. He worked, but not at such a frantic pace. After the initial impetus of the Cantor tour, his career climb had slowed. He made an occasional guest appearance on television, and he made the move from RCA's Bluebird Label to the Black Label, recording four singles for them, with more scheduled. The first—"Where in the World" and "A Little Bit Independent"—had not done extremely well; nor had the second—"Warm Kisses in the Cool of Night" and "Night Wind." The third single did somewhat better—"Just Say I Love Her" and "Give a Broken Heart a Chance to Cry." The fourth had not yet been released.

Eddie, of course, was impatient; things were not moving fast enough to suit him. But Milton knew that this was an important gestation period; he had been working quietly gaining the respect and confidence for his client among the important people in the recording and entertainment world. Great progress had been made, but it wasn't visible yet. It all didn't happen quite the way it did in one of those 1940s movie musicals.

But Milton's advice paid off in June of 1950. Singing star Fran Warren, who was to play a major engagement at the Riviera, was ill. Bill Miller needed someone to play the engagement, and he needed someone fast. Remembering Eddie Fisher had done the private party for him, he called Milton Blackstone, and asked, "Can Eddie go on in twenty-four hours?"

Eddie's first reaction was, "No!"

Milton was astonished. "Eddie," he shouted, "this is the chance of a lifetime."

"I can't get ready that fast," Eddie protested. "I haven't even got a tuxedo." He was torn by all sorts of mixed feelings. He knew it was a great opportunity, but it was so fast, and he would be substituting for someone else. Finally, he relented, grinning at his manager, "And besides, I'm scared to death."

The twenty-four hours of preparation for the engagement at the Riviera would have satisfied even the corniest and most sentimental of show biz movies. Bernie Rich recalls Eddie's excitement: "He was a nervous wreck; so were Joey and I, getting him ready. Our boy was taking over for Fran Warren, and he was as unsure of himself as a cow on a city street.

"We spent most of the day running around trying to find him a tuxedo. Then we had to get him the necessary alterations. Finally, we took the tux to our apartment, and hung it in the closet. Then we tried to calm the butterflies in Eddie's stomach by taking him out for some food.

"When we returned to get him dressed, we were locked out.

"Puzzled, we sought our landlady. Then we remembered our rent was past due. We tried convincing her that Eddie was the star of tomorrow, but all she extended was a grubby paw. After Eddie's face registered hopeless despair, the mother instinct in her stirred, and she handed us the key."

They got Eddie dressed, and then had time to rehearse him for an hour. Eddie was frightened at having to go on without more preparation. This would be the first time that his act would be reviewed, and it would be reviewed by all the major entertainment newspapers. The possibility that he had to make it or break it had him scared. Also, he was sharing the bill with comedian Henny Youngman, and that meant celebrities were bound to be present.

Among the songs that Eddie sang that night were "I Wanna Be Loved," "Wanderin'," and "There's No Tomorrow."

The reviews could easily be called raves. *The New York Times* said "Merely wonderful, a sensational singing voice and style."

Eddie was overjoyed; at last he was a hit.

RCA Victor released Eddie's fourth single on the Black Label—"Thinking of You" with "If You Should Leave Me" on the flip side—and the rapid sales caused it to zoom high up on the charts. The recording company quickly set up dates for more recordings.

With all best intentions, Eddie determined that he was going to work as hard as humanly possible to merit his new stardom. When he wasn't working, he was rehearsing; when he wasn't rehearsing, he was making plans. As a result, when the engagement was over, Eddie landed in Mount Sinai Hospital with influenza. The newspapers took note of that fact, and Eddie was surrounded by cards, letters, telegrams, flowers, books, and admiring nurses. He read and reread his notices, and wondered if he were dreaming.

But this time he was not. Club offers poured in from everywhere. "Thinking of You" climbed higher and higher on the charts. And—most astonishing of all—fan clubs burst into bloom, not just in New York and New Jersey, but all over the country.

When Eddie was well on the way to recovery, Milton Blackstone determined it was time to give his new star some fatherly advice. He reprimanded Eddie for pushing himself too hard. He agreed that Eddie had to work hard to deserve his fans, but there were other areas Eddie ought to concentrate on right now. For one thing, Eddie's education was lacking; not only had he dropped out of high school, he was also ignorant of the world. All Eddie knew about was Eddie and singing. He was going to be meeting all sorts of people soon, and he had to be conversant in other things. Did Eddie know there was a war starting in Korea? Did it ever occur to Eddie to try reading *The New York Times?* Not just Eddie's review in the *Times;* the whole paper.

Also, Eddie was going to have to get his teeth fixed, and fast, because Milton was planning a major engagement at the Paramount. Eddie's teeth were in terrible shape; he would probably need a complete capping job—the whole mouth—and at a cost three times as much as it should because it would have to be done so quickly.

Eddie took Milton's advice to heart. He had the capping done. But, reading *The New York Times* was going just a bit too far. He made an effort, but without any success. He found it just too dull.

As for Milton's advice about pushing himself too hard, Eddie forgot that as soon as Milton had said it.

With the end of 1950, prizes and awards of recognition began coming in, most significant of them all being *Billboard* magazine's "Most Promising Male Vocalist of 1950." He was also beginning to be called upon for benefits and charities.

Early in 1951, Eddie returned to the Paramount Theater. This time he didn't have to go begging Bob Weitman on his knees. This time, he went in as a star earning $5,000 a week. His billing appeared both on the marquee and on an enormous banner above the marquee. The movie listing read: "Dick Powell, Rhonda Fleming, *Cry Danger.*" Among those on the living show billing were: Russ Case and his Orchestra; Eddie Fisher and the Five DeMarco Sisters.

And the fans who lined up outside the theater weren't coming to see the movie either; they were coming to see and hear Eddie Fisher, the new singing sensation.

As usual, things had a way of coming between Eddie Fisher and "happily ever after." America, through the United Nations, had become involved in the Korean Civil War; young men eligible for the draft were being called up as quickly as the government could operate. One of the earliest entertainers to be called was Eddie Fisher, cutting short his engagement at the Paramount Theater on March 6, 1951.

5. Mr. Fisher Goes To War

The United States came out of World War II considering itself the guardian of democracy throughout the world. To avoid a recurrence of world war, it considered American aid—both financial and military—of the utmost importance. The nations of the world had set up the United Nations to attempt to achieve this, but the United States considered its efforts would simply insure that the United Nations succeeded.

It was through a United Nations peace force that the United States became involved in the Korean "Civil War," a war some say was fomented by Communist China, a country not a member of the United Nations because the United States refused to recognize it. Like so much about the 1950s, illusion became reality, and the truth became an explanation of how to encircle the illusion without touching it.

The illusion was that the United States was in Korea as part of the UN peace-keeping effort, to quell a civil dispute between the North and the South. The truth was the United States was engaged in a war with a nation it would not recognize. And it may well have been that nation's main object in waging the war.

Most people in the United States had no idea of what that war was all about. It seemed simply a natural extension of World War II. Fascism had been an ideology different from democracy; communism was also different. If the fascists were out to conquer the world, so then must the communists. And it was America's responsibility to prevent that, no matter where.

Eddie Fisher was as patriotic as the next guy; he was quite willing to serve his country, but he hated to forsake his newly-won career. Milton Blackstone assured Eddie that there was nothing to worry about. He would see that Eddie's army career would serve to enhance his singing career. Eddie would be able to continue to record singles for release carefully during the two years he would be out of the country. As Eddie "marched off to war," another single was released—"Bring Back the Thrill" and "If It Hadn't Been for You"—and it did even better than his last single had done, selling more than half a million copies.

Photographers and reporters were present for each step of Eddie's entry into military service. The articles and captions in newspapers and fan magazines indicated that Eddie was being treated like any other draftee. And indeed, during basic training, Eddie got no favors.

He picked up his uniform at Ft. Devens, Massachusetts, and was sent to Fort Hood, Texas, for basic training assigned to the 16th Armored Engineer Battalion, under Sergeant Robert Abrahms. He had to get up at 3:30 A.M. for K.P. duty just like all the other privates, an hour he used to go to bed as a civilian, so he had some difficulty in adjusting to the new schedule.

To his credit, Eddie asked for no favors, and wanted none. He was aware that the other G.I.s were watching every move he made, waiting for him to act like a celebrity. But Eddie didn't. He acted no different from others, and he did everything they had to do.

However, he could not change the fact that he was a celebrity. The other men would have made it absolute Hell for Eddie if he had tried to act like one; but the fact he did everything they did made him acceptable. For example, when they had to take a fourteen mile hike with backpacks and rifles, Eddie did it just as everybody else did; greeted by cheers from his division when he returned to base. If the men had to run four miles, he did it like everyone else, astounded that his green fatigues turned white from the loss of salt.

One thing about Eddie Fisher at this stage of his life: he was still malleable; he took orders or directions well. He was still a kid emotionally, and he looked for authority to tell him what to do. He fit very well into the army, and he even enjoyed it. It is even safe to say that he benefitted from the hardships and the camaraderie of his basic training, and he fully expected to spend his entire two years as a buck private, going to Korea as a fighting man.

But that did not fit in with the plans made for him. Milton Blackstone had assured Eddie his career would not suffer from his military service; in fact, Milton had been at work to see that Eddie's service could be turned to good advantage.

The big singing idol of the 1940s, Frank Sinatra, had been able to build his career by being on the homefront during World War II. (To his credit, Sinatra had tried to join up, but he was 4F.) In this age of mass communications, Milton had figured out how Eddie could appear both on the homefront and on the battle front.

The largest number of single recordings of Eddie Fisher's career were issued during the two years he was in military service—a total of eleven in 1951, and nineteen in 1952. Some of them called attention to his military service—such as "My Buddy" and "Goodby G.I. Al" and "I'll Hold You in My Heart." A great many of them made the charts; and he had a second single to go above the half-million mark—"Turn Back the Hands of Time," with "I Can't Go On Without You" on the flip side.

Eddie also had his first million-selling gold record in 1951—"Anytime."

Eddie was aware of this part of Milton's plan before setting off for Fort Hood. He learned about the other part after his basic training was over.

When Eddie was called to report to the commanding officer at Fort Hood, had he done something wrong, was he going to be reprimanded? Had there been too much publicity about him, too many distractions from the business of training for war? On the contrary, he was informed, he was being reassigned to an entertainment unit, with which he spent the remainder of his time in the military service appearing with the U.S. Army Band.

It had all been arranged by Milton Blackstone, master promoter, who had convinced the Army that Eddie Fisher entertaining in uniform would be the best public relations and recruiting gimmick the Army could have. Of course Milton was right; the arrangement not only benefitted his client; it benefitted the Army as well.

In all innocence, Eddie was able to face reporters and say, "Seems somebody at the Pentagon decided I'd be more useful as a musician than as an engineer." In a way, he was happy about the development, but in another way, he was not. He liked the position he had achieved among his peers, and he felt somewhat guilty about not being shipped off to the front with them. When Milton explained that he was serving his country much better this way, he accepted it, but not wholeheartedly.

Eddie's doubts seemed to be confirmed as the weeks went by without any mention being made of his going to Korea to entertain the troops. The appearances scheduled for him were all in the United States. He travelled around the country singing for the recruitment program. He sang to sell defense bonds. He sang to get people to donate blood for the blood plasma program. He even sang to fight cancer, polio, and muscular dystrophy. But he wasn't doing anything for the individual fighting men who were making real contributions to the war.

Eddie found himself appearing on television just about as much now as he had been before he entered the service. He was a guest on the Milton Berle show; he did charity telethons, and he appeared on Jane Froman's *USA Canteen* a number of times. On one occasion, he and comedian Jack Carter appeared with Jane to help select the official U.S. Army song; on another occasion he appeared so that Jane could present him officially with his first gold record, for "Anytime."

Frustrated that he was not at the front, Eddie tried to do more and more, becoming a real glutton for work. It was Jane Froman who first noticed that he was straining his voice, and she spoke to him about it and to Milton Blackstone as well. Operating on anxiety and frustration, Eddie couldn't heed her advice.

Finally, Eddie saw his chance to get what he wanted. He was to visit army installations and hospitals in the Washington, D.C., area. A local disc jockey asked Eddie if he would like to meet President Truman. Eddie promptly answered "yes."

The meeting between the two was not a particularly comfortable one. The young singing idol who found reading *The New York Times* a terrible chore and the no-nonsense President could find very little to talk about. Truman opened the conversation with, "How is my favorite Pfc?" and the conversation almost stopped there.

In the awkward silence that followed, with the shy Eddie completely tongue-tied, Truman walked toward the window and commented, "I don't know what the hell I'm doing here." When Eddie didn't offer any suggestions, the President asked, "What do you want to do while you are in the army?"

Eddie finally found his tongue: "I would like very much to go to Korea, sir."

That struck a responsive chord with the President; he could understand and sympathize with that sort of request. And what's more, he could do something about it. "I would like to see you go to Korea," Truman said, "and not just there but all over the world as well."

A few days later, it was settled: Eddie was going to make a world tour to entertain U.S. troops all over the globe—Japan, Hawaii, Wake Island, Alaska, the Aleutians, Europe, Iceland, Greenland, and most important, Korea. Eddie was delighted; at last he could feel he truly was serving his country.

It proved to be a frantic, wearying pace, but Eddie Fisher seemed to thrive on it. He went to the front lines, singing for as few as 100 G.I.s in some places and as many as 20,000 in others. Sometimes there would be a stage and bleachers; sometimes Eddie simply stood in the mud and sang to the men seated on a hill or on the ground. He did some shows in the rain from the back of a truck, often without a microphone, often without even musical accompaniment.

At times he found the men so starved for entertainment that he had to stay for twenty to twenty-five songs before they would let him go. A favorite with the men was one of Eddie's hits, "Bring Back the Thrill." They asked for it again and again.

But Eddie did more than sing on his tour. He talked to his fellow G.I.s and gave them news from home. Many of them gave him their girls' names and telephone numbers to call for them when he got home. Eddie did call as many as he could when he returned. The response was not always what he hoped. Often, when he would say, "Hello, this is Eddie Fisher," the girls wouldn't believe him and would hang up.

When Eddie appeared at army installations, local talent was used to fill out the bill. Eddie was amazed there was so much good talent among the enlisted men. He did his best to offer them helpful advice, and invariably he would be asked to listen to songs aspiring GI songwriters had written.

If Milton Blackstone had been worried about his valuable singer risking his life on the front lines of Korea, he shouldn't have. Eddie had never felt better in his life. He even gained weight, filling out his skinny 5 foot 8½ inch frame to 132 pounds, a gain of a good ten pounds.

And Joan Wynn, still Eddie's girl, was encouraged by the emotional growth she saw in Eddie's letters. She told her friends, "His letters are showing a lot of maturity. I think he is growing up and is going to come back the man I want him to be."

Joan wrote to Eddie just as often as he wrote to her. It began to appear they would finally achieve a strong sharing relationship where each could carry his or her own weight. She looked forward to Eddie's return to New York and to a future of happiness together.

Eddie was doing his best to live on his Pfc. pay of $99.37 a month, but he never seemed to be able to manage. However, Milton was able to send him money, since the royalties from his recordings were now paying him $330,000 a year. In his second year of military service, one hit song after another soared up the charts —"Thinking of You," "Wish You Were Here," "Outside of Heaven," "Lady of Spain," "Even Now," and many others.

Milton Blackstone was working very hard for his client. All of the planning that had gone into creating Eddie Fisher had been his. From start to finish, it proved to be a work of genius, a masterpiece of promotion and public relations. He was continually making contacts, and building, and planning for the day when his client would get out of the army. And Milton did not neglect the most minute of details. When he or members of his staff were in the vicinity of record shops, they went in to check the stock of Eddie Fisher records. When they found it lacking, they placed an order, which prompted the store manager to stock the records for other customers.

When in 1952 Eddie's parents finally decided to be divorced, Milton managed to keep unfavorable publicity from leaking out. Eddie naturally was upset about the break, but he understood when his mother explained that "It was an impossible situation." He knew all too well what their marriage had been like.

By December of 1952, about four months before Eddie was to return to civilian life, Milton had everything planned and settled. Eddie was on a European tour at the time—England, France, Germany, and Iceland—so Milton flew to London to meet with him. Milton had business in Portugal, and—he explained to Eddie—he figured he might as well pay a social call on his young friend. But Milton had other things in mind as well.

He took Eddie to the Palladium, where Jack Benny was appearing. With all of Milton's contacts, he quickly managed to have Eddie meet all the right people associated with the Palladium. Before they left, Eddie had been engaged to appear there the following year.

Playing the Palladium in London was considered a milestone for an important entertainer, much like playing the Palace in New York. In reality, it wasn't all that it was cracked up to be, since a star had to appear with so many other acts that he almost lost his identity in the shuffle; but it had prestige value and lots of promotional possibilities.

Just to make sure his client would not be a total unknown in England, Milton stopped into a few record stores and placed some orders for "that American singer, Eddie Fisher."

Naturally, Eddie was curious to know if Milton had any prospects lined up for him when he got home. Proudly, Milton announced, "Don't worry. You're going to sing for Coca Cola."

Eddie didn't understand, so Milton explained that he had recently had a meeting at the "21" Club with Pat Weaver, president of NBC, and with Robert Sarnoff, chairman of the board of RCA. A representative from Coca Cola was also present. They wanted to sign Eddie to do a television show; and it seemed logical that Coke would be the best sponsor for him. Dinah Shore represented Chevrolet and Perry Como was on for Chesterfield cigarettes, so they couldn't very well look to an automobile company or a cigarette company for a sponsor. Since they anticipated an audience of 15 million teen-age girls, Coca Cola seemed the logical sponsor.

Milton also informed Eddie that he would be able to continue his engagement at the Paramount.

As it turned out, Eddie's two-year engagement with the U.S. Army proved to be a veritable triumph. Special Services awarded him a special tribute stating "Eddie Fisher was a credit to the U.S. Army . . ." and that "His untiring efforts in entertaining the combat forces were appreciated and lauded by all who came in contact with him."

Milton wrote a statement for Eddie to deliver, saying, "I feel only humility for honors I've received . . ." and "The fighting men deserved them more."

However, Eddie also gave his own message to newsmen, "The army taught me discipline. It showed me how to do things that had to be done, how to get along with people, but mostly how to accept things as they happened to me and make the best of the situation."

At 8:00 A.M. on April 10, 1953, Eddie was discharged from the Army. Three hours later, he was on the stage of the Paramount Theater in New York, in civilian clothes, singing for his adoring fans.

6. E-d-die! (Or Not A Dry Seat In The House)

By the time Eddie Fisher returned to the Paramount stage as the main attraction, the 1950s were in full swing. General Dwight Eisenhower, called "Ike," had only recently been inaugurated, and his fatherly aspect was much more in keeping with the illusions of the times than had been the frankness and bluntness of his predecessor. The American people wanted out of Korea, and Ike had promised he would bring the boys home. In April of 1953, truce talks were well under way, and the armistice would soon be signed.

Millions of homes now had television sets, and they were watching them religiously, so much so that the motion picture business feared for its life. Quickly, the movie moguls started cogitating for ways to attract the audiences out of their homes. They had to give people something different; they came up with 3-D and with wide screen. For awhile, the gimmick worked.

Soon after Eddie's triumphal return home, Grossinger's held a "Welcome Home, Eddie Fisher, Day" in his honor. Family and friends and celebrities were all invited. There was to be a banquet and a golf tournament. That evening, after the tournament, Eddie was presented with a trophy that read, "Best left-handed singer playing in the tournament." It was a very sentimental occasion, but also a shrewd publicity maneuver by Milton Blackstone. He had to remind everyone that, although Eddie had hit the top at the Paramount, he had been "discovered" at Grossinger's.

In this era of hype and hoopla, the outward signs, the show put on for the public press, was more important than the truth or reality. Eddie was assigned the same publicity agent at NBC that Perry Como had, so a fast friendship was worked up between the two top singers for publicity purposes. Pictures of the two constantly appeared in fan magazines, and they often made public appearances together. But they did not really become close friends: they both realized they were somewhat in competition with each other. And they were, as later music polls would show.

The phenomenal success that turns a real person "overnight" into a mythological figure is difficult for anyone to adjust to, even someone who has worked and struggled for that success for a lifetime. Eddie Fisher's success at the Paramount and on *Coke Time* gave him a strong case of overconfidence.

Just about every record that Eddie made in 1953 hit the charts as soon as they were released, and often the record companies couldn't determine which of the records' two sides were the most popular. Among the biggest hits of that year were, "How Do You Speak to an Angel?," "Downhearted," "Just Another Polka," "I'm Walking Behind You," "With These Hands," "Oh, My Pa-Pa," and "Many Times."

Coke Time, which had premiered both on radio and on television on April 29, 1953, was a big success. Shown twice a week for fifteen minutes, it was carried by 702 television and radio stations, a record in popularity for those years. Its theme song was "Anytime," Eddie's first gold record.

The producer was Sonny Werblin, of MCA (Music Corporation of America). Monte Proser, of the Copacabana, acted as production advisor. Don Ameche was the first emcee; but, when he left to do a Broadway show, he was replaced by Fred Robbins, a popular disc jockey on New York station WINS.

But it was Milton Blackstone who designed the format of *Coke Time,* insisting that Eddie be the last person the audience would see at the close of the show. The camera came in for a close-up, and the home audience saw the boyish face of Eddie Fisher. Most of the words Eddie spoke were especially written for him by Milton Blackstone.

Eddie received $7,000 a week for *Coke Time.* Added to his income from other appearances and from records, he was doing extremely well. His annual income was somewhere around $300,000.

Most of the reviews for his television show were good. Those who found fault with it were critical of the one thing Eddie had already realized from kinescopes. His big problem was finding out what to do with his hands. Eddie sums up his early performances as "Just awful." However, one critic who pointed out that Eddie was in danger of being called "old-fashioned," summed it up more objectively: "Young Mr. Fisher just stands there and sings."

With his constantly renewed energy Eddie had to find something to do when he wasn't working, so he began to develop a very busy and active social life. He still occasionally saw Joan Wynn, but their lives were growing so far apart after Eddie's success that their romance began to settle into a friendship. He was now dating other girls from the Copa line, and occasionally taking out female singers and starlets.

And he developed a great many other friendships as well. Once, after they had both had injections, Eddie and songwriter Alan Jay Lerner partied for three days without stopping.

Both Milton and Eddie were determined that Eddie would keep a good and close relationship with his fans. To do this, Milton leased one entire floor of the RCA Building, and he hired an enormous staff to take care of relations with the 10,000 fan clubs that had been set up. One of the young women hired was named Rona Burstein, later known as Rona Barrett. Another was Judy Tannen, who later went on to become personal manager for Eydie Gorme and Steve Lawrence.

Milton coached the secretaries on how to advise official club members where they could buy Fisher souvenirs; he worked up brochures that covered every detail of organizing a fan club—membership drives, the best places to meet, how much to charge for dues. The secretaries answered 3,000 letters a week, and sent out about the same number of photographs personally autographed by Eddie Fisher.

Eddie did not read his mail; that would have been a physical impossibility, even with his extra energy. But he did autograph all the photos. And Eddie did not overlook the secretaries themselves.

One of them, Jane Shacknow, recalls an occasion when she had given Eddie a stack of photos to autograph. It happened to be her birthday; later, she found one of Eddie's photos on her desk signed, "Thanks for putting up with me, Eddie."

Because of Milton Blackstone's careful planning, Eddie was to go straight from his phenomenal success at the Paramount to play the Palladium in London. Eddie would be there well in advance of the Coronation to became an established hit in England.

Milton had seen to it that Eddie's records were selling in Britain, and that his reputation preceded him across the Atlantic. He was a big hit at the Palladium, and he would prove to be an even bigger hit at the Coronation.

There was a party at the Dorchester Hotel, the Red, White, and Blue Ball, honoring the American notables who were in London for the Coronation of Queen Elizabeth. The American Embassy called Milton to ask if Eddie would appear at the ball to entertain.

"Do you want to play a benefit?" Milton asked Eddie. "Princess Margaret will be there."

At first Eddie said, "no," but he thought for a moment, and then asked, "Who did you say was going to be there?"

When Milton repeated that Princess Margaret would be at the ball, Eddie changed his mind and agreed to appear.

Before Eddie came out to perform, he received a note backstage; it was from Princess Margaret, telling him that she was a fan of his, and that he should not be nervous. The note asked that he sing, "Outside of Heaven," one of his hits from 1952, which had appeared as the flip side of "Lady of Spain." It was a gracious gesture, and it gave Eddie confidence for his first appearance before royalty.

He stayed onstage for forty-five minutes, accompanied by the Palladium orchestra, singing song after song, to tremendous applause. The audience loved him, and he loved the responsive audience, but he knew he could not stay on forever. When he had finished singing the last words of "Outside of Heaven," the applause was deafening, led enthusiastically by the lovely Princess Margaret Rose.

Backstage, Eddie received word that Princess Margaret would

E-D-Die! (Or not a Dry Seat in the House) 73

like him to join her table. As Eddie walked across the ballroom floor toward the table occupied by the Princess and her royal entourage, he had butterflies in his stomach. When Princess Margaret rose to greet him, the entire room leaped to their feet. Eddie, not knowing royal protocol, was bewildered, thinking it must be some kind of ovation he was getting.

However, the graciousness of royalty can handle just about any situation. Princess Margaret put Eddie at his ease instantly by praising his performance, confessing that she was such an ardent fan of his that she had all his recordings, even those that were not yet on sale in London.

Eddie asked why she particularly liked "Outside of Heaven." Margaret answered that she really didn't know; it was such a sad song, and she generally preferred happier ones.

Eddie remained with the royal party all evening: and, as the hours wore on, the formality was dropped. Eddie danced with the Princess, and later everyone sat on the floor chatting the way young people did back home in the United States.

Afterwards, reporters all wanted to know what Eddie thought of the Princess. He commented on her "warm, compassionate eyes," on her dignity and poise, adding, "I had the feeling I was speaking to someone one thousand years old."

Back home in America, everyone asked Eddie about Margaret; some even conjectured about the possibilities of a romance. When Eddie Cantor asked about the experience, Fisher was the bashful shy boy, responding, "Imagine me meeting an English princess."

Cantor quipped back, "Imagine her, meeting an American Prince!"

Indeed, by the summer of 1953, when Eddie returned from England, that is what he had become. He traveled with an enormous entourage (which on the trip to England had included Dr. Max Jacobson), and he was continually acclaimed by his fans, who behaved like clamorous royal subjects.

Copa chorus girl with young Eddie

The Jane Froman Show, U.S.A. Canteen.

Kate and Joseph Fisher at Eddie's second Paramount opening.

Eddie and brother Bunny — 1953.

Base pay of Pfc. Fisher was $99.37.

Francis Cardinal Spellman.

Princess Margaret.

Bill Miller, Riviera owner, signed Eddie to contract.

Mr. and Mrs. George Montgomery (Dinah Shore) with Eddie.

7. The All-American Boy And Girl

In the 1950s, the American public deified love. They also deified sex, but they kept the two separate. And the persons they selected to deify as the gods and goddesses of love and sex were as different as it was possible to be. The deities of sex were almost all women—Marilyn Monroe, Elizabeth Taylor, Jayne Mansfield, Sophia Loren, Gina Lollobrigida, Anita Ekberg. It was preferred that they remain single; if that was possible, the public at least asked that they not stay married long. Everything possible was done to accentuate the physical sexual nature of these stars; the styles of clothing accentuated breasts and buttocks; and faces were heavy with makeup.

There were single male deities as well, but their sexual nature was not emphasized as much—at least until Elvis Presley came along. They were attractive—such figures as Tab Hunter, Rock Hudson, James Dean, Paul Newman—and they did appear without their shirts whenever possible, but sex, as far as men were concerned, had to remain unspoken. They were, after all, potential love symbols.

The deities of love were supposed to be pure and innocent, and they invariably appeared in pairs—Robert Wagner and Natalie Wood, Desi Arnaz and Lucille Ball, Fernando Lamas and Esther Williams, George Montgomery and Dinah Shore, Roy Rogers and Dale Evans. Eddie Fisher and the girl of his choice would eventually come to head that list.

In 1954, Eddie's fans began to press for information about his love life. During the preceding year, they had accepted the many fan magazine articles that suggested he didn't have time to think about love yet; all he could do was to adjust to his new success. However, they would not accept that explanation for long. Just about every interviewer who questioned him asked about his love life, and Eddie always answered evasively.

He was still seeing Joan Wynn occasionally, but that romance was waning, and Eddie's managers wanted him to keep quiet about it. If Eddie spoke about it at all, he had to speak of it as past. Singer Jill Corey who had appeared frequently on *Coke Time* developed a heavy crush on Eddie, and even took to walking up and down his street hoping she would run into him. But Eddie wasn't responding; she just wasn't his type.

One interviewer, after Eddie gave the usual evasive answer about his love life, asked a different question: "Who do you think is the most beautiful girl in the movies?" Without hesitating, Eddie responded, "Elizabeth Taylor, of course." Then he added as an afterthought, "And Debbie Reynolds; she's very cute and versatile." He had as yet met neither of these women. And, it seemed, he had no desire to meet them. When Merv Griffin invited Eddie to attend a party at a friend's apartment—trying to persuade him by explaining that Elizabeth Taylor, just divorced from Michael Wilding, would be there—Eddie refused.

It may have been because so many people were interested in his love life that Eddie chose to pick his female companions himself and to keep them secret. Most often, his dates were spur of the moment things, possibly to escape publicity. An example of this occurred in September of 1953, when Eddie was serving as the honorary parade marshal at Atlantic City's Miss American Pageant. At the festivities, Eddie and Lee Ann Merriwether, the 1952 Miss America, found they were being ignored, so they quickly slipped out together and went for pizza.

Eddie truly did have too much on his mind to get himself tied down to one girl. He was so busy and so active that marriage would be more a handicap than a help to his career. Freedom was essential to his maintaining his schedule of appearances.

The longer Eddie held off from connecting himself with a

steady girl, the more his female fans clamored for him. A number of them found out that he had an apartment in the Essex House on New York's Central Park South, and they would gather there in groups. When their screaming began to disturb his neighbors, Eddie pleaded with them to leave because they were getting him in trouble. However, his fans continued to stand there, especially when they knew he might be coming in or out, only now they stopped pushing and screaming.

His fans were generally considerate of his requests. During the early months of the televising of *Coke Time,* he had asked them not to shout and scream, because it would create sound problems. They obeyed his wishes and sat very decorously and appreciatively throughout the televising.

However, *Coke Time* began to have space problems. In the beginning Eddie was given a small studio at NBC, but the numerous set changes—one for each musical number—meant that he quickly outgrew the studio. In 1954, *Coke Time* was assigned a larger one, and this one had no seats for an audience. At Eddie's request, NBC installed a special glassed-in booth where a small group of Fisher fans could watch and scream to their hearts' content.

At the end of 1953, Eddie had come in a close second to Perry Como in the *Cash Box* poll for the top male vocalist. The vote had been so close—only a fifty vote difference—that *Cash Box* decided to award a "Second Top Male Vocalist of 1953." By the end of 1954, Eddie easily won the top vocalist award. And by that time, he was also inalterably linked romantically with a young actress named Debbie Reynolds.

A few of Eddie's hit songs for 1954 were: "Anema E Core," "A Girl, A Girl," "Green Years," "I Need You Now," "Fanny," and "Count Your Blessings."

This last—"Count Your Blessings"—proved to be one of Eddie's most memorable hits, one that achieved for Eddie one of his proudest moments. In October of 1954, he was asked to entertain at a dinner in New York, commemorating the 300th anniversary of the first Jewish settlement in America. The principal speaker for the evening was the President of the United States, Dwight D. Eisenhower—"Ike." The President's speech was intended as the only portion of the evening to be televised. Eddie sang, "Count Your Blessings," and left the podium to listen to Ike's speech. As the President took his place, the television cameras started. However, Eisenhower did not go into his speech; instead he turned to Eddie and asked, "Eddie, please sing one more chorus of 'Count Your Blessings' for the television audience."

Eddie was thrilled. With genuine sentiment, he has said, "That was one of my biggest thrills, my own personal command performance."

But the biggest Eddie Fisher hit of all time has to be "Oh, My PaPa." It sold 890,000 copies in the first four weeks it was on the market. It earned him another gold record, and its final total in sales was more than four million.

Because of the record, in June of 1954, the National Father's Day Committee honored Eddie and his dad, presenting them with an enormous cake. Swiss composer, Paul Burkhard, who wrote the song, visited Eddie on *Coke Time* and presented him with a music box that played the song. Proudly, Eddie told Paul at the time, "I'll never sing a song I like any better as long as I live."

Eddie had to sing "Oh, My PaPa" so often on *Coke Time* that Monte Proser ran into problems trying to think of original set designs for it. Eddie sang it on his show eight times while it was on the charts.

Fisher records were selling at an average of 60,000 to 70,000 a week. Although Milton Blackstone was managing his business for him, Eddie was responsible for supporting a great many people. At least thirty different people—recording executives, song pluggers, managers, advertising executives, newspapermen, television producers, friends, and just plain hangers-on. Eddie increasingly found that he was not the boss. They were. They owned him; he could hardly call his life his own. In addition to those thirty, there were a great many others he had some obligations to. His Christmas list numbered 8,000 people. Of that number, 3,000 were "business associates."

Eddie felt that he had to keep all those people happy. Whatever they asked, he felt he had at least to try to do. After only a year of top stardom, the pressure was beginning to get to him. He never had a quiet evening at home. His apartment was always filled with people, usually people connected with career business, who looked upon his home and his dressing room as their clubhouse. He couldn't go anywhere without fans surrounding him, tearing at his clothes and trying to touch him.

This was the price of fame. And so, perhaps, were the injections of Dr. Max Jacobson, which he was having to turn to increasingly.

He had sought fame, and, now that he had it, he realized there were some values to be an ordinary person—an ordinary All-American Boy, which was ironically what the press painted him as being.

Eddie's meeting with the All-American Girl should have been set-up by his managers and press agents, but it wasn't. In fact, if the choice had been theirs, it wouldn't have happened, at least not so soon, because it interfered with the smooth operating of the Eddie Fisher business.

Eddie was to play an engagement at Hollywood's famed Cocoanut Grove in June of 1954, and he had to go out in April to prepare for it. While he was in Hollywood, he stopped at MGM to see Gordon MacCrae, who had stood in for him on *Coke Time* while Eddie was in London. Gordon was on a lot filming *Oklahoma*. While they talked, Gordon showed Eddie around the lot. On the next lot, the movie *Athena* was being filmed. MGM executive Louis Pasternak was there, and Gordon introduced him to Eddie.

Looking over the *Athena* set, Eddie noticed an attractive girl wearing rehearsal tights, no make-up, and with her hair in pin-curls. Eddie was amused because she was sitting there trying to learn to play a harp that was twice as big as she was. When she looked up and saw Eddie watching her, she blushed.

Louis Pasternak noticed the exchange of eyes, and he explained that she was the film's star, Debbie Reynolds. Would Eddie like to meet her? Eddie acknowledged that he would.

Actually, Eddie and Debbie had run across each other before, in Washington, D.C., though the meeting had not been very memorable for either of them. Eddie, who in uniform, had made a much bigger impression on Debbie's mother, and she was the one to recall the event. It had been early in Eddie's military service, and he and Debbie and Carleton Carpenter had appeared together to entertain the servicemen who were in Walter Reed Army Hospital.

On this second occasion at MGM, Debbie was still not overly impressed with Eddie Fisher. He seemed much too shy and serious. Debbie explains, "I've always liked the athletic, start-the-laugh type."

Eddie, however, was impressed with Debbie. Later, talking to disc jockey Johnny Grant, he asked, "Do you happen to have Debbie's private phone number?" When Grant replied that he did, Eddie beamed. "You do? Could you help a fellow out and give it to me? I'd like to call her."

Eddie did call Debbie at her parents' home in Burbank. She still was not overly impressed, especially since Eddie told her he had to leave the next day for New York. But she was courteous to him; and, when he asked if it would be all right to call her from New York, she responded, "I'd like that," thinking she would never hear from him again.

Debbie had just turned twenty-one when she met Eddie. Most of her dating had been set up by the studio publicity staff, dates with such stars as Tab Hunter, Robert Wagner, and Carleton Carpenter. Despite the fact that Eddie seemed shy, she rather liked the idea he had taken the trouble to get her number and call her. It was a bit more romantic than what she was accustomed to.

Debbie had achieved stardom at a young age. Born Mary Frances Reynolds in El Paso, Texas, on April 1, 1933, she had moved with her parents and her older brother Bill to Burbank, California, when she was eight years old. Her father was with the Southern Pacific Railroad, and he had been transferred.

She was truly the All-American Girl next door. She was from a middle-class family, one very close and loving. Their religion was Baptist, and they lived in an ordinary comfortable middle-class home in Burbank, noted for being a middle-class town. Up until Debbie won the 1948 Miss Burbank Beauty Contest and received a six-month contract at Warner Brothers with an option that was picked up by MGM, Debbie was the typical American teenager.

She played the French Horn in the high school band and learned to twirl a baton. She was, however, overzealous in her twirling prowess; and, during a parade, she tossed her baton too high, with the result that the wind blew it through a window of the Glendale City Hall. The window happened to be to the Mayor's office.

Debbie's first movie appearance was in *The Daughter of Rosie O'Grady,* in 1949, at the age of sixteen. This was quickly followed in 1950 by *Three Little Words, Two Weeks with Love,* and *Mr. Imperium.* But she really hit it big in 1951 with *Singin' In The Rain.* She had made a total of ten pictures before she met Eddie Fisher.

Success had not changed Debbie. She was determined that it would not. She continued to live at home with her parents in the same house they had lived in before her success. Only two things were changed—she had persuaded her dad to install a swimming pool in the back yard, and to enlarge her closet to make room for a larger wardrobe.

There was something about that attitude that Eddie Fisher admired and respected. Debbie was not like those clinging, climbing types he was used to in New York, who sought out the glamor and excitement. Debbie was beautiful and talented, but even more fantastic, she had as much domesticity as his own mother.

To Debbie's surprise, Eddie did call her from New York. Typical of Eddie's insecurity, he began with, "Hi, do you remember I said I'd call?" After chatting for awhile about "How are you" and "How's the weather" they set their first date, June 17, 1954, when Eddie would be back in California for the Cocoanut Grove appearance.

Eddie had not bothered to tell Debbie what June 17th was; perhaps he assumed she knew. She did find out only a few days before, when reading *Variety.* It was announced that June 17th would be Eddie's opening at the celebrated nightclub.

This threw Debbie into a panic. "Oh, Mom," she gulped and showed the article to her mother. The first thing she could think of was that she would need something special to wear. She and her mother debated at length over what color dress she should wear, what kind of hair-do, what kind of make-up, and how much of her bosom should show.

Debbie's mother made most of her clothes, and she immediately went to work on a beautiful red lace outfit for the occasion.

Eddie may or may not have realized that this public occasion was not the ideal one for a first date with someone he truly liked. Whether he did or not, it proved to be a very wise step when he called Debbie after his arrival in Hollywood to ask her to a party at the home of Dinah Shore the night before his opening. Even though they were seated at the same table with Jerry Lewis and his wife and with Jack Benny's wife Mary, they had an opportunity to get to know each other. Perhaps it was because they were at that table Debbie got to see that Eddie had a sense of humor after all. He took a great deal of kidding from Jerry about Debbie.

If the Cocoanut Grove opening had been their first date, Debbie might never have seen Eddie again. Seated at the table with them were a large group of Eddie's "managers," and they monopolized Eddie. No one paid any attention to her at all. If Debbie was in the least impressed with Eddie, she was not impressed at all with his "cronies." In fact, very few people in Hollywood were.

Columnist Hedda Hopper's response was typical, though she was the only one gutsy enough to talk about it in print. She first saw Eddie when she was having lunch at Romanoff's in Beverly Hills. Eddie came sauntering in, surrounded by two characters who looked completely out of place in the swank surroundings. She asked her tablemate, "Who in the name of God is that? And who are those terrible looking men with him?"

"That's Eddie Fisher," her friend responded. "And they're his handlers."

"Handlers?" the famous Hedda guffawed. "Is he a prize fighter? I'd heard he was a singer."

If Debbie had been wise in the ways of the music business, she would have been able to see the handwriting on the wall. But, in the beginning, she did not see a great deal of Eddie's business associates. After the Cocoanut Grove, Eddie took a vacation; he had been working a frantic pace for over a year and a rest would do him some good. He had rented a house in Beverly Hills for the summer; he could relax in the California sunshine and have a good time.

He spent most of that time in the company of Debbie Reynolds, her family, and friends. He was deliriously happy, enjoying precisely the kind of life he had been missing in the mad rush of his career in New York. It was the real but ordinary life of family and friends. The Reynolds household was such a warm and loving one, Eddie fell in love with it instantly, and the Reynolds family reciprocated. The warmth was not displayed excessively, but was best displayed by Debbie's dad, who—when he liked someone—called him "Hoss." Eddie quickly merited the term.

Eddie and Debbie's relationship developed the way young people's relationships developed all over the country. They played records, danced, went swimming, barbecued hamburgers in the back yard, and went for long drives in Eddie's convertible. They spent a lot of time with Debbie's group of friends, "the gang." It included Robert Wagner, Lori Nelson, Terry Moore, Tab and Jeff Hunter, Piper Laurie, and just as many non-celebrities. Their gatherings and jaunts were informal, and Eddie loved the casualness of it all. Nobody was a celebrity; they were all simply friends, just like ordinary groups of young people all over America.

On one occasion, the gang drove up to Lake Arrowhead to swim and water ski. Eddie had never been on water skis before, but he was willing to try. When the group got back to the Reynolds home that evening, Eddie's face was glowing. It was the most radiant expression Maxine Reynolds had yet seen from Eddie, and she had some natural motherly curiosity. She asked. "What's with this cat-that-ate-the-canary look?"

"I didn't fall down, not once," Eddie exclaimed boyishly, and Maxine Reynolds sighed with relief.

When Eddie drove up in front of the Reynolds house, the neighborhood kids would crowd around his car, but not because he was Eddie Fisher. It was his car they were interested in—a fantastic Thunderbird convertible. He enjoyed the kids enthusiasm so much, he would pull up on the street and yell, "Who wants a ride?" and all the kids within hearing would hop into the car, and take a ride around the block.

Debbie delighted in Eddie's boyish pleasures. In the beginning, she thought him too shy and lacking in a sense of humor. But the shyness disappeared quickly, and his sense of humor appeared when he began to relax. He would do the kind of zany things that she adored, and loved to do herself. Once, when they had been dining at the Sportsman's Lodge, out in the Valley, a woman from New Orleans approached Eddie in the parking lot and begged him to come to New Orleans so she could hear him sing. Eddie burst into song in the parking lot; when he had finished an entire number for the lady, he announced, "There, now I don't have to come to New Orleans."

On another occasion, Debbie and Eddie were driving down Wilshire Boulevard, almost always so heavy with traffic drivers have to stop at nearly every traffic light. The occupants of a car in the next lane recognized Debbie and Eddie, so Eddie serenaded them all the way down Wilshire, while Debbie roared with laughter.

The publicity the couple received that summer was excessive to say the least. Their first date was reported in all the gossip columns and fan magazines; after that, their every move received attention. On July 4, only two weeks after their first date, headlines appeared announcing they had been secretly married in Las Vegas. Of course they had not been married, and both Debbie and Eddie had a good laugh about it. But it had an effect on them nevertheless: they both liked each other; they had fun together; but they had no idea whether they were in love or not. Because of the gossip, they had to consider it a possibility.

The great misfortune for Eddie and Debbie was that they *looked* so perfect together. They were the epitome of the All-American boy and girl, and they became deified instantly by the public. They were the American lovebirds as no other couple since Doug Fairbanks and Mary Pickford had been. The American public, in love with love, could not get enough information about their activities.

The 1950s were given to excess in many ways, and gossip under the guise of news was no exception. Newspapers and magazines that muckraked into the private lives of celebrities were springing up out of all sorts of dark corners, and the American public bought them, smuggled them home, and read them when nobody else was looking. A lot of what appeared in them was fabricated, a lot was true; and very few people—possibly including the writers—knew for certain what was true and what was not. The public, at least, didn't care; nothing about Eddie and Debbie was too private or too personal; they had to know it all.

The publicity had its effects on the couple, and upon their respective families. Eddie had told his mother before this, "Mama, don't believe any rumors you hear about me unless you hear it from me." In the beginning, when people asked her about the romance, she just shrugged and answered things like: "That's nice, isn't it?" or "Very interesting, I'm sure." or her real clincher, "It's healthy for young fellows to go out with girls, I hear."

When Eddie did feel he was beginning to get serious about Debbie, he called his mother from California to tell her. The moment he began speaking to her, she knew something was different. She asked, "What's the matter? You got a stomach ache from all those California oranges or something?"

"No, Mama," Eddie answered. "Don't worry. I've been eating well." Then she could tell there was a happy note to his voice. "I've met a girl, Mama. I've met a girl and she's really something."

Immediately, Kate Fisher knew. "Is it this Debbie Reynolds everybody here in Philadelphia has been telling me about these last few weeks?"

Eddie told her that it was. "I think I might be in love with her, Mama. I might ask her to marry me."

Although Kate Fisher had no idea who Debbie Reynolds was, she was overjoyed. "My Sonny Boy, getting married!" But she endeavored to be a good mother, adding, "If you think this is the right girl for you, then I know she is the right one." She paused, and then added, "I wish I could meet her, Sonny."

Eddie assured her, "You will, Mama, you will. Just as soon as possible."

After they finished talking, Kate went into the kitchen where Eddie's sister Eileen was having lunch. She told her fifteen-year-old daughter about the conversation and asked, "Eileen, do you know what she looks like, this Debbie Reynolds?"

Eileen was so excited she couldn't finish her lunch, but her mother wouldn't let her answer. Kate just kept asking more questions. "Do you know anything about her? Have you ever heard of her?"

"Mama," Eileen was finally able to break in, "Don't you ever look at any of the magazines I bring home?" When her mother confessed that she didn't, Eileen exclaimed, "Honest to pickles," and rushed out of the room, returning with a stack of fan magazines. Pointing to the first picture she could find, she announced, "This, Mama, is Debbie Reynolds."

Looking at the picture of Debbie, Kate thought she would like her very much; it was such a sweet, pretty, smiling face. However, the thought did occur to her that Debbie didn't look Jewish. No matter, that was her Sonny Boy's business. As soon as Eileen was out of the house and Kate was alone with the fan magazine, Kate held up the picture of Debbie and said, "Hello."

The Reynolds family liked Eddie very much. He was sweet, kind, and considerate. Their only reservations about him were based upon the difference between his religion and Debbie's. Jewish and Baptist were about as different as you could get, except for maybe Moslem and Jewish. However, Debbie had a very strong will of her own. They knew she would decide for herself whether or not religion would make a difference.

The Reynoldses at least had the satisfaction of seeing the truth for themselves. The romance was blossoming right under their noses. They knew instantly when a piece of gossip was a fabrication.

To make things easier for his mother, Eddie called her before he left Hollywood and put Debbie on the phone so they could at least speak to each other. The first words Kate heard from Debbie were, "Hi, this is Debbie. May I call you Mom? I've heard so much about you. Eddie has such fun telling me about his family, I just can't wait to meet them."

Kate liked the voice she heard from the other end, but she was still anxious to see the person behind the pictures and the voice. For that, however, she would have to wait awhile.

Eddie and Debbie's idyllic summer together had to come to a close. Eddie had to get back to New York and to business—a new season of *Coke Time,* new recording sessions, more public appearances. Debbie had more work to do on *Athena,* and then had to go on to complete *Hit the Deck.* They both felt the separation would be good for them. They both felt head-over-heels in love, and they had already talked about marriage. The fan magazines were rushing them toward that end; but they both needed to get some objectivity about the subject, some time to think.

It was arranged that Debbie would come to New York when she was free of her motion picture commitments. She would be able to see Eddie on his home "turf" and meet his family.

The meeting with the family went very well.

As soon as Eddie knew what day and time Debbie and her mother were flying to New York, he called his mother and asked her to arrive early in the morning to be sure to be there when Debbie arrived. Excitedly, Kate and Eddie's sister Janet flew to New York, meeting Eddie at the airport with plenty of time to see him before Debbie's plane got in.

As Debbie's flight was announced, they were surrounded by newsmen and photographers. Eddie let out a jubilant, "Yippee!"

The suspense built as everyone waited to catch sight of Debbie Reynolds. As soon as Debbie spotted Eddie, she went rushing into his arms, while photographers snapped pictures.

Quickly, Debbie turned to Kate and said brightly, "Hi, Mom!" Kate could not help but be happy and proud about the delightful and beautiful girl her son had chosen. Instantly, she was charmed by Debbie.

After photographers had gotten all the pictures they wanted, Eddie, Kate, and Janet went with Debbie and her mother to their hotel suite. Over cookies and tea, the families let Eddie and Debbie do most of the talking; but soon, Debbie excused herself and took Eddie's mom off to talk and get acquainted. She told her, sweetly and openly, "Mom, when I met your Eddie, something inside of me said love. I'm in love with Eddie for a lot of different reasons. But one of the reasons I love him most is that your Eddie hasn't forgotten that he was once a little person. He hasn't forgotten who he was."

Kate gave Debbie a kiss, took her hand, and proceeded to tell her about her Sonny as she knew him. She confessed she had always hoped he would marry one of the Jewish faith, but she would try not to let that matter now.

Kate and Janet spent three days in New York getting to know Debbie and her mother, an enjoyable three days. They returned happily to Philadelphia, pleased about Eddie's choice.

As soon as he got a few days free, Eddie took Debbie to Grossinger's to see his second home, and to meet his second "family." Again, everything went well. Debbie relaxed into the Grossinger family warmth and hospitality; they often sat around a piano, Eddie singing and Debbie harmonizing. Occasionally, they would do a few dance steps (with Eddie still an elephant) or do a comedy routine. They were both just as much in love as they had been during the summer in California.

At the end of September, the couple had another brief separation while Eddie flew to Newfoundland to make a personal appearance. However, he called Debbie from there to tell her to expect a surprise when he flew home the next day. Debbie and Lori Nelson made plans to welcome Eddie home with a home-cooked dinner in Joey Forman's apartment.

That evening, soon after Eddie arrived, he took Debbie aside into another room where they could be alone for a few moments. When they came back into the room, Eddie had his shy look on his face, and Debbie was beaming happily with tears in her eyes. She extended her left hand to display a seven-carat diamond ring.

It may have been that Fanny—the toy poodle Eddie had given Debbie—knew something the happy couple didn't. In surveying the apartment, Fanny found the gray suede ring box and chewed it to shreds before anyone could discover it.

Debbie's parents announced the engagement on October 19, 1954, and the press outdid themselves with ecstatic articles and gossip. Everyone wanted to know when the marriage would take place, but no one could give the gossip columnists any hints.

Eddie Cantor gave an engagement party for Debbie and Eddie in Hollywood, and the movie stars and celebrities attended as if it were the opening of a major motion picture.

As it turned out, that was the pinnacle of the couple's happiness. Debbie soon began to notice obstacles to their marriage.

The first inklings came from some of Eddie's fans. The young girls loved the idea of the Fisher-Reynolds romance, but many of them were not too keen on the marriage.

Eddie had to play an engagement at Palisades Amusement Park in New Jersey, and Debbie accompanied him. A group of Eddie's fans were waiting for them, carrying signs protesting the marriage. The announcement also seemed to hurt his record sales. When "A Man Chases a Girl (Until She Catches Him)" came out, with Debbie as the mystery voice in the background, it turned out to be his first single in almost two years not to be a hit.

Eddie's managers began to get worried, and some of them began to throw obstacles in the way of his marriage. It seems fairly certain that none of this interference came from Milton Blackstone. Milton tried to be kind and gracious toward Debbie; and she in turn respected Milton as the man responsible for Eddie's success. But others—it is not quite sure who—began to plant doubts in Eddie's mind. Some created problems simply by not going along with what Eddie wanted.

The most obvious example of this was when Eddie asked that *Coke Time* be transferred to one of the NBC studios in Los Angeles so that at least some of his work could be done from his home. His request was refused. Then there was the problem of Eddie's schedule; there seemed to be no flexibility; Eddie began to discover that he had little to say about trips he would be making all over the United States, and throughout the world. There just wouldn't be time, some of his "brain trust" seemed to be saying, for him to get married.

Debbie wanted a big wedding, one with a set date, planned well in advance. However, Eddie could not get a firm commitment of a free date in his schedule.

Admittedly, part of the problem was with Eddie. Although he had matured a great deal since he had first entered the army, he was still not a strong and decisive man. The decisions that had turned him into a success had all been made by others. Anytime Eddie was confronted by a choice, he seemed unable to make up his mind. First he would say no, then change his mind back and forth until the decision was made for him. Anytime he himself did anything on his own initiative, it was done on the spur of the moment.

When things really began to break down between Eddie and Debbie, he pointed to this fact and suggested they elope. To Debbie, who had always dreamed of a big wedding, this was not a satisfactory solution.

As the second thoughts set in for Eddie, Debbie also found herself having second thoughts. Eddie told Debbie about Dr. Max Jacobson and about the vitamin injections he was receiving, and recommended she take them. Debbie refused; and she began to question whether Eddie ought to be taking them either.

As 1955 came in—the midpoint in the decade of the fifties—they were both beginning to realize that they were rushing too rapidly toward marriage. They hadn't even known each other a year. They needed more time.

But the press didn't want to give them more time.

Al Jolson's widow receives gold record of Eddie's "Goodbye, G.I. Al." Harry Akst, Jolson's former accompanist, watches.

Eddie with Louella Parsons.

Two Aries personalities who influenced Eddie's life: Milton Blackstone and Debbie Reynolds.

8. The Marriage That Almost Wasn't

It was almost a year between the engagement of Eddie Fisher and Debbie Reynolds and their marriage. It was an on-again, off-again romance, followed every step of the way in the press and the fan magazines. It was a wearying year for the couple—and for the public as well. For, by the time Eddie and Debbie were finally married, most of the people who might have cared didn't care any longer. Although very few of the real reasons for the delay ever made it into print, the public microscope was able to see Debbie Reynolds as a valiant and much-abused young lady, while Eddie Fisher came off as a heel, if not actually a fool. The public blamed Eddie for the whole mess, and they wished he would hurry up and make up his mind one way or the other and get it over with.

However, Eddie was not to blame; or, if he was, it was only indirectly. Certainly, Debbie was not at fault. At fault was Eddie's business, a business that he was the center of but not in charge of.

The romance began to crumble in London. Eddie was scheduled to play two weeks at the London Paladium in April, with a Royal Command Performance at Blackpool on April 13, 1955. Eddie wanted Debbie to go with him, but he knew that he had a vicious schedule in England, and he warned Debbie that his free time would be limited. Debbie, perhaps wanting to see what it would be like to share Eddie's life, insisted that it didn't matter; she wanted to go anyway, and her mother would accompany her.

In Eddie's offices in New York, there was considerable confusion about when Debbie and her mother would be there. Up until the last minute, no one was absolutely sure if they would arrive in time to fly to London with Eddie and his associates, Milton Blackstone and Harry Akst. But Debbie and her mother did make it.

They arrived on a foggy Sunday morning, March 27. The airport was jammed with hundreds of teenagers who were just as eager to see the couple as were the fans back home. There were also a great many members of the British press, even though the London newspapers were on strike.

Curiously, the song that had failed to catch on in America—"A Man Chases a Girl"—was the number one hit in England. Eddie delighted in that, and he was determined to use it in his act.

He opened at the Palladium on March 29, to a jammed house. Every seat was taken (except the royal box), all the standing room was sold, and hundreds had to be turned away at the box office. As usual at the Palladium, he shared the bill with a number of other acts—eleven to be exact. However, when Eddie came on, he was met with screams and applause. He sang song after song, and the audience loved him.

The hit of the evening, however, was "A Man Chases a Girl," which required a female mystery voice from backstage. The audience recognized the voice instantly, and they screamed, "Where is she? Come out, come out!"

Debbie came onstage in a short blue evening dress, exchanged a few words with the audience, gave Eddie a kiss, and made her exit. That brief moment brought down the house.

Eddie's schedule was, as usual, a grueling one. He was doing two evening shows each day plus matinées on Wednesdays and Saturday. His one free day from the Palladium was Good Friday, but he had been scheduled for two shows at a theater in the suburb of Tooting. At every free moment between shows, Eddie was scheduled for press conferences or interviews or meetings with his fan clubs. He spent long hours signing autographs.

Debbie also had to spend long, dull hours in his dressing room between shows, waiting patiently while he rested or looked over a new song, talked to agents and song-pluggers, or gave interviews. Just standing or sitting around was tiring for her, and it was often irritating, because there were times when she was sure he could be alone with her but he didn't make the effort.

Eddie, with the aid of his injections, never seemed to get tired, or even to need sleep. Debbie apparently began to have her doubts about how her marriage to Eddie might be. More than Eddie's faults, more than his business associates, those injections might prove to be their greatest obstacle. She tried to talk to Eddie about them, but he wouldn't discuss the subject: they were harmless; and he needed them to keep going at such a hectic pace.

Eddie did not want to neglect Debbie in London; he was torn between his love for her and his business obligations. He had warned her what it would be like before she had decided to accompany him, and there was no way he was going to allow his business associates to accuse him of shirking his responsibility.

He did make an effort to make the trip enjoyable for her when he could, but even then he knew everything was not truly the way he would have liked them to be.

Debbie's twenty-third birthday was April 1, three days after Eddie's opening at the Palladium, and Eddie planned a surprise birthday party for her. And since Milton Blackstone's birthday was April 2, the party would also be in his honor. There would be two huge cakes for the occasion: Debbie's would have twenty-three candles, and Milton's would have one.

(It is interesting to note that both of Eddie's important partners at this stage of his life were born under the sun sign of Aries. Astrology attributes strong-mindedness and self-will to Aries natives. Those born under this sign are also supposed to be noted for their wit, their determination, and their persistence, being also noted for a quick temper coupled with a willingness not to hold a grudge. Aries natives also are notorious for liking to talk.)

Eddie managed to keep the birthday party a secret by confining the guest list to a handful of intimate friends, his press representative, a few members of the press, and three fan club presidents. He also invited singer Johnny Ray as a special surprise for Debbie. It was held at London's Embassy Club, and Eddie lured Debbie and her mother there under the guise of taking them out for a night on the town.

When Eddie, Debbie, and her mother entered the Club, the band played "Happy Birthday," and everyone stood up and toasted her and Milton with champagne.

Earlier, Eddie had given Debbie several gifts. One was a ballerina pin with pearls and diamonds on the dancer's skirt and hair; another was a beaded evening bag; and, just before leaving for the party, he had given Debbie the largest bouquet of flowers he could find in London. At the party, he told her that a set of white luggage she had been wanting would be at the airport waiting for her.

Debbie did get to see a bit of London while she was there. Eddie managed to get enough time free to take her out to a few nightspots, going twice to the famed Café de Paris. They took a ride atop the double-decker buses, and they paid a visit to Westminster Abbey. Eddie also hired a car, and they took a quick drive into the countryside around London, making a detour to show Debbie one of his favorite spots, the Great Fosters.

But it was not, generally speaking, a romantic two weeks for Debbie.

The highlight of the trip was Eddie's appearance at the Royal Variety Performance in Blackpool, the first Command Performance ever held outside of London. It was a benefit to raise money for a benevolent fund; all of the 3,000 seats had been sold, and all newspaper people had to stand throughout the show.

Eddie's act was the longest, lasting eleven minutes; and he again sang "A Man Chases a Girl," with Debbie helping from backstage.

After the performance, Eddie was presented to the Queen and the Duke of Edinburgh, along with all of the other entertainers. When he was presented to Philip, the Duke of Edinburgh asked, "Are you really going to marry Miss Reynolds?"

Eddie's immediate answer was, "I sure am, in June." When asked if Debbie would continue with her career, Eddie's reply was, "Yes, certainly. She's a great artist, and I don't think our marriage should interfere with her career."

Afterwards, Eddie and Debbie put in a brief appearance at the carnival dance at the Winter Gardens Empress Ballroom, held for those who had been unable to get tickets for the performance, and then at 3:00 A.M., they left by sleeper for London, where they boarded a plane for Portugal.

After the two hectic weeks, Eddie and Debbie were at last able to have some time together, in peace and quiet, resting in the sunshine on the beach, and going sightseeing. They attended a dinner party with Cole Porter their first evening, and had a delightful time. But they spent only two days in Portugal before hopping off to Paris to do some shopping, then headed to New York.

Debbie and her mother then returned home to California to make plans for the June wedding, but she returned, she said, "feeling blue." She said later it was a mistake making the trip to London with Eddie. However, it had shown her something—that Eddie's superhuman schedules would make for some difficulties in married life. He had warned her about this, but now she had seen for herself. She had thought his working schedules were more like her schedules as a movie actress—intensive work on a picture for several weeks, and then lots of time off before the next picture. But it was not; Eddie's schedule was work, work, work, all the time.

They set a wedding date—June 17, the anniversary of their first date together. It was growing very near, frighteningly near, and they still had so many things to work out between them. However, the gossip columnists and the public were clamoring to get it over with.

Before they had left for London, Eddie and Debbie had settled on several major points—the wedding date, June 17, followed by a honeymoon of almost three months, the period when Eddie would have his vacation. Because they had been so happy together in California, they would buy a house there as home base; to go along with this, Eddie put in a request to transfer his *Coke Time* show there.

After returning to New York, Eddie conferred with his managers to see if all this was still possible. As it turned out, it was not. They explained that moving his television show to California would mean uprooting several families. While they could obtain some of the necessary staff there, the most important people would have to come from New York. Eddie wouldn't want to put his New York staff out of work, would he? Eddie protested; he had often had to commute back and forth between Los Angeles and New York; surely some sort of schedule could be worked out for the television staff to commute as he had done. His managers agreed that commuting was possible, so they set up a schedule for each of his television shows to be done from a different city around the country—none of them to be from Los Angeles.

Furthermore, Eddie's summer vacation was cancelled; his managers booked him for the entire two-and-a-half months he hoped to have his honeymoon in Europe. Nor would he even get his wedding day off, at least not the whole day.

There was nothing Eddie could do about it. His managers had signed contracts that committed Eddie to appearances. They had the legal right to do this; if Eddie refused to follow through, he would be the one in breach of contracts; he would be the one to be sued.

When Eddie reported this to Debbie, who was already downcast after her experiences in London, she was as furious as Eddie was. He suggested they elope, but Debbie refused. They were at an impasse, and they decided the only thing they could do was to cancel the wedding, to postpone it indefinitely.

The reason given by Eddie's managers for changing his summer schedule was Eddie's faltering popularity; he had to get out and reestablish contact with his fans. They claimed Debbie had hurt his popularity, and they pointed to his record sales as proof: of the songs released in 1955—"Dungaree Doll," "A Man Chases a Girl," "You Gotta Have Heart," "I'm Always Hearing Wedding Bells"—the only successful one was "You Gotta Have Heart," the only one that did not relate in some way to Debbie Reynolds.

If Eddie's popularity had sagged before, it plummeted after his wedding date was cancelled. In the public eye, Eddie was blamed for everything. Columnists suggested that the wedding was never really intended to be, that the whole romance between Eddie and Debbie had been engineered as publicity for Eddie Fisher. Eddie very correctly pointed out, "That would seem a little absurd, because it was clear she was doing more to hurt my career than to help it."

The columnists had seen something, however; it was just that they had been unable to identify it accurately. The romance between the couple was real; when Eddie's managers saw the publicity emanating from it, they decided to play it up. They released those recordings that related to Debbie; when they flopped, it seemed evident that the publicity was not benefiting Eddie's career. They then hoped cancelling the wedding would serve to stimulate business. They proved to be wrong again.

In the ensuing weeks, there was as much publicity as any public figure could want, but it was all of the wrong kind. Everyone concerned tried not to talk about it. When Milton Blackstone was asked, he invariably responded, "I don't speak for Eddie Fisher." When Debbie was asked, she clammed up and insisted it was a very private matter. On one occasion when Eddie was asked what his future plans were, he paused so long the interviewer interjected, "Take your time—we're on the air for another hour." Finally, Eddie was able to say, "I want to keep my private life to myself."

In the midst of all the hubbub, Debbie decided she had to do something to occupy her time, to get away. She had cancelled her film schedule expecting to be married and taking her honeymoon. Now she had nothing to do but think about the whole mess. Hurriedly, she made arrangements to take a USO tour to entertain the American troops still stationed in Korea.

Before she left, she announced very calmly, "All my life my parents have taught me to seek happiness. I feel that my happiness will be with Eddie. My two weeks in Korea will give us both time to do a lot of thinking. This is a decision about our whole life, and we can't make it right away. Eddie and I are very much in love. We will have to decide whether to get married immediately, as we had planned, or to wait."

Eddie responded to an interviewer, "She called me one day and said she was going to Korea. I was surprised." To another, he gave out the statement that he didn't know how long their engagement would last or whether they would ever get married. "I just don't know," he said sadly.

And things were not much better after Debbie returned. Eddie spoke to the press again, dejectedly, "We still love each other. I don't think this is the time to get married. There are just too many problems that have to be worked out. I don't know when we will get married; I just don't know when or if . . ."

Everyone connected with the situation hoped the public curiosity would fade. And it did, even though some columnists endeavored to keep it alive. Perhaps eventually a resolution could be worked out that would satisfy everyone.

Perspective was what everyone needed, but unfortunately perspective cannot truly be gained in only a few weeks or a few months. Certainly, Eddie could not admit at age 27 that he was still too immature for marriage. And Debbie, as mature as she was at age 22, was also a romantic, and she could not admit the possibility that love did not always find a way out of any predicament.

As for Eddie's "brain trust," they simply had no way of knowing that the slip in Eddie's popularity had nothing whatsoever to do with what they or Eddie were doing. Caught up in a decade they helped to create, they had no idea it was about to overwhelm them. If they had really analyzed things, they would have realized Eddie's fans did not remain the same age year after year. True, he was a "teenage idol," but any set group of teenagers remain teenagers for no more than seven years—from age 13 to age 19—though the hard-core fans are generally ages 15 to 18. Most of Eddie's original fans were beginning to grow out of their teens by 1955. To remain on top, Eddie would have needed to accept growing older along with his audience, or he would have to have adapted himself to the demands of a new generation of teenagers.

The first signs of the new wave appeared in 1954. A hit song entitled "Shake, Rattle, and Roll" was the precursor of something called "Rock and Roll," that hit full force in 1955 with "Rock Around the Clock" and "Dance with Me, Henry," and then the explosion of a new superstar in 1956 named Elvis Presley, who monopolized the charts with songs like "Blue Suede Shoes," "Don't Be Cruel," "Heartbreak Hotel," and "Hound Dog."

Established singers, managers, and publicists met the new phenomenon with astonishment and bewilderment, unable to understand why and how it could be such a rage among the youth, even though they themselves had paved the way for it. It was in keeping with the approach of "excess," and with the tradition of screaming teenagers. Only this new craze finally gave teenagers something to scream about, a blatantly sexual rhythm and an idol who undulated his pelvis suggestively.

As for Eddie Fisher, his fans couldn't really have cared less whether he married Debbie or not. He was only doing what they themselves were growing up to do after all, only they were doing it quietly and without fanfare.

Eventually, Eddie and Debbie had the good sense to realize that the only way they would ever be married would be to do it quietly, without fanfare. And surprisingly, it was Eddie who had the courage and audacity to make the necessary steps, defying everybody. The result was a compromise between Debbie's wishes for a big wedding and the wishes of those who did not want a wedding at all, but at least it satisfied the principals—Eddie and Debbie themselves.

At the end of the Labor Day Weekend in 1955, Eddie paid a surprise visit to Grossinger's. It was Monday, the holiday crowds were leaving; and no one expected him at all. He came to see Milton, and the two of them sat up all night in the clubhouse and talked. It was the moment of decision for him, and he had to have someone to turn to. Milton was the only one he had ever been able to turn to for fatherly advice. Milton was the only one he could turn to now.

Eddie asked, "Whatever am I going to do?"

Milton was sympathetic, but he explained that he could not make Eddie's decision for him, explaining, "You have to make this decision all by yourself. No one can make it for you. Don't listen to anyone Eddie, not even her. Especially not her."

Throughout the night, Milton obstinately refused to offer further advice, but he was willing to listen, to be a soundingboard for Eddie just to get all his thoughts and feelings out in front of him.

They were still there talking when the janitors came in to clean up. Eddie was determined to see Debbie again. He called her, arranged for her to come to New York, and he left his boxer

"Junior" with Milton to dog-sit, as Debbie was not fond of the animal.

Debbie arrived in New York on Friday, September 16; Eddie met her and took her to Grossinger's for the weekend. Left alone together without outside interference, they still had just as much fun; they still seemed to love each other just as much as always. They returned to New York for the Rocky Marciano-Archie Moore fight at Madison Square Garden on Wednesday, sitting down front and yelling like two schoolkids, having gotten to know Marciano while he was training at Grossinger's.

After the fight, Debbie called her mother to tell her she would be staying on for a few more days. Eddie called Milton and said, "I want to get married; can you help us get a license without the usual waiting period?"

The next night, Debbie called her mother again, this time giving her instructions: "Come right to New York. Call Jeanette (Johnson); tell her to bring her maid-of-honor dress. And get me something to wear. I don't have anything here to wear. Get something from the studio, and get me some white shoes, and bring my veil. And mom—don't tell anyone. Especially not the studio. We're going to get married Sunday. Can you be here by then?"

Her mother was astonished. "How am I going to get a dress from your studio without telling them why I want it, and suppose Jeanette can't come with me tomorrow?"

"Oh, details!" Debbie exclaimed. "You fix it, Mom. Don't forget the veil." As an afterthought, she added, "I'll get you a room at the Plaza."

In Burbank, Mrs. Reynolds had to pause a moment to take stock of everything she suddenly had to do. The first thing she did was to call Debbie's best friend, Jeanette Johnson, who was a high school gym teacher, to see if she could fly to New York to be maid of honor. Luckily, Jeanette would have no problem getting some time off from school. Then, Mrs. Reynolds searched the house and found the veil that Debbie had borrowed for the June Wedding that had not taken place.

The most difficult task was to get a wedding dress. The dress that Helen Rose (from M-G-M) had designed for *The Tender Trap* was hanging in Debbie's locker at MGM. Somehow Mrs. Reynolds had to get the dress out of the studio without anyone knowing.

While she was off on her secret mission, Mr. Reynolds called Debbie's brother Bill to tell him the news. Bill wanted to talk to his mother to get the details, but his father had to explain, "You can't. She has gone out to steal Debbie's wedding dress."

Which is a pretty accurate description of what Mrs. Reynolds was doing. The guard at the MGM gate knew Debbie's mom, so he let her in without asking for an explanation. She parked in the back of the building and sneaked in to the locker area. She quickly took the wedding dress, and silently slipped out the same way she had come in.

Arriving in New York the next day, Mrs. Reynolds and Jeanette were met at the airport by Eddie's valet, Willard Higgins, with Eddie's limousine. They were taken to the Plaza Hotel and checked in. They didn't hear from Debbie until the next day, Saturday, September 24, when Debbie called from Grossinger's to inform them, "We decided to stay up here for it, Mom. It's so pretty, and everyone is so nice to us. The hotel cooks said they will make us a cake, and Jennie's daughter, Mrs. Elaine Etess, who just moved into her new home, asked us to use her house for the ceremony. Also, we can't get married until after Sunday because Sunday night is the beginning of Yom Kippur, and Eddie wants to observe the holiday and go to temple. So if you come up here now, you can spend Monday keeping me company, and we'll get married Monday night."

In a haphazard and hurried manner, the wedding was taking shape. However, they did not yet have someone to conduct the ceremony, so Paul Grossinger called Judge Lawrence Cook of Sullivan County to ask, "I've got two friends who want to get married Monday evening. Will you perform the ceremony?"

"No," the Judge responded, "I'll be busy; "I'm going to a clambake."

Paul then had to explain that his friends happened to be Eddie Fisher and Debbie Reynolds, but they wanted to keep it a secret.

"Oh," came the judge's response, "then I'll do it."

There was so much to do, and it all had to be done so secretly, that nerves were wearing thin. Jennie Grossinger had ordered flowers from the local florist, but she couldn't tell why she needed them, so she had to do the decorating herself. A large buffet was set up in the dining room of the Etess home, with a hugh centerpiece of purple daisies and yellow roses with candles inside. The living room was filled with flowers, and a white cloth was spread as an aisle from the stairs to the living room, where the ceremony was to take place.

A special table was set up for the huge five-tiered wedding cake which had taken the cooks 24 hours to make.

When Mrs. Reynolds and Jeanette Johnson arrived at Grossinger's on Sunday, the day before the wedding was to be held, Debbie and Eddie were both looking somewhat haggard and worn.

"There's been so much happening to us so fast," Eddie explained, "we don't know if we are coming or going. And keeping it a secret, too. . . . Everyone keeps saying, 'What are you so up-in-the-air about?'"

"You look as though you could use a nap," Mrs. Reynolds clucked over her daughter. "A bride is supposed to be blushing, not flushing."

Suddenly, after seeing her mother, Debbie remembered that her clothes were back in New York; she had intended that her mother would bring them. After much consternation, arrangements were made to have them flown up to her.

Dr. Jacobson was at Grossinger's, and that evening he was to give Eddie an injection. As soon as Debbie saw the needle, she turned white. "He doesn't need that," she blurted out.

"Do you have a medical degree, young lady?" Jacobson barked back at her.

Defensively, Debbie could only say, "No, of course not."

"Then I'll decide what's best for my patient," Jacobson cut her down with a superior air, and proceeded to give Eddie his injection.

From sheer exhaustion, Debbie went to her room at the Etess home and passed out.

Eddie went to the temple on the resort grounds to hear Kol Nidre.

The wedding was set for eight o'clock the following evening.

Eddie spent most of the day in temple; Debbie slept until four in the afternoon, then got up to try on her dress, which her mother had had to make a slight alteration on. It fit perfectly. However, Debbie suddenly discovered her mother had brought two left shoes.

With little time left, a pair of white shoes had to be found in Debbie's small size four. Because of the time of year, no one at the hotel had white shoes, and most stores in the area were closed for the religious holidays. Finally, however, someone came up with a pair of size four white shoes, embroidered.

By 7:45 P.M., Debbie was fully dressed, wearing Jeanette's garter for something blue, the shoes for something new, the veil for something borrowed, and she put a brand new dime into one of her shoes.

However, ten minutes later, and only five before the ceremony was to take place, Debbie was told she might as well sit down for awhile. Eddie's mother had called to say she was stuck in traffic and would be late. Eddie had called his mother on very short notice, and she had decided to drive up for the occasion with Eddie's brothers and sisters.

At 8:15, she called again to say she was still on her way.

In separate quarters, the bride and groom were beginning to suffer from the strain. Despite the attempts at secrecy, more than a hundred reporters and photographers were outside. Debbie suspected George Bennett, Eddie's publicity manager, had tipped them off, but she decided to accept the *fait accompli* and permit one of them inside for the wedding; he would have to share his photos and information with the rest. However, there were to be no photos of the service itself.

The reporters and photographers who waited outside began to shiver in the cold September night. As the delay grew longer, Paul Grossinger suggested they wait in the shelter of the basement of the Etess house.

Finally, at ten minutes before nine, Eddie's mother and family arrived. Judge Cook immediately started the proceedings. A trio of musicians promptly begin playing "Moonlight and Roses," while the parents of the bride and groom were seated.

Suddenly, someone realized the candles in the aisle were unlit, so he quickly ran down the aisle and lit them.

Eddie and Milton (who was acting as best man) and Jeanette Johnson took their places.

The trio began the wedding march, and Debbie walked down the aisle. The ceremony itself took place with no more problems. When Eddie kissed the bride, Debbie heaved a great heavy sigh that everyone was able to hear.

At the reception, Eddie noticed that his mother was crying, so he went over to her and said, "Smile, Mama, smile."

She looked at her son, sniffed, and informed him, "Look, I am happy, and I am enjoying myself—so I am crying."

George Bennett approached the couple, smiling, and asked, "Well, how do you feel?"

Simultaneously, Eddie and Debbie both answered, "Oh, I couldn't feel happier." Then they looked at each other and laughed, and Eddie commented, "Since the two of us are now one, we couldn't feel happier."

At long last, they were married—for better, or worse. Although neither of them expected the "worse," it came.

Debbie and "Fanny."

Young love.

The Eddie Cantors gave a star-studded engagement party for Debbie and Eddie.

Eddie's stepfather, Max Stupp, with his new family.

Newlyweds pose with two who symbolize Eddie's career: Milton Blackstone and Jennie Grossinger.

September 26, 1955.

The perfect family.

"Bundle of Joy" advertisements.

9. Trouble

Eddie and Debbie did not have the European honeymoon they wanted. In fact, their honeymoon was stolen in between Eddie's appearances and rehearsals. They were supposed to have spent their wedding night at the home of a friend of Jennie Grossinger's. However, they slipped away from the reception and disappeared until Eddie's appearance at a Coca-Cola bottlers' convention in Washington, D.C. They hopped from there to New York for a World Series game at Yankee Stadium, leaving early so Eddie could rehearse for his television show.

Their "honeymoon" slipped into routine married life without much of a change of pattern. Debbie had to return to California to finish a movie, *The Catered Affair;* Eddie was unable to accompany her because of work. It was left to Debbie to find a house, which she did; they moved into it on December 13, 1955. It was a big, sprawling Pacific Palisades estate, made of brick and shingles, set on six acres in the midst of a wooded area extending from the highway a half a mile to the ocean. The house came complete with a swimming pool, a number of utility buildings on the grounds, and a walk-in fireplace in the living room.

When Eddie was finally able to join Debbie in the house, problems began for both of them, first in a mundane way, with a difference in sleeping and waking schedules. Eddie was a night person in the habit of sleeping late. Debbie, because of her work, was a day person, having to get up early to be on the movie sets by dawn. Whenever they wanted to do things together, she would have to stay up late or he would have to get up early.

Eddie was used to big city night life, entertaining and doing late-night shows. Aided by injections, he would go out for jam sessions with the boys after Debbie went to bed, not returning until the wee small hours of the morning.

Sometimes Debbie would be getting up about the time he came home. She would sit in her dressing room at the studio and think about him alone in the house. Feeling guilty, she would call up and ask, "Eddie are you all right? Did you find everything when you got up? Do you want to know where something is?" Then she would hang up the phone and complain to anyone who would listen, "Really! A wife's place is at home!"

But, in the beginning at least, they had their love for each other.

To liven up the house, they had Eddie's full-grown boxer, Junior, and Debbie's poodle, Fanny. To liven it up further, they got a boxer pup. Debbie often quipped, "The only other thing we'd like around the house to make the menagerie complete is a baby." And behind the joking Debbie seriously wanted a baby. She would have her wish very soon.

The real difficulties Eddie had early in their marriage did not stem from Debbie or from their relationship. They centered around Milton Blackstone with whom he had a business disagreement; everyone denies it had anything to do with the obstacles placed in the way of Debbie's and Eddie's marriage.

Whatever it was, during the early months of 1956, he and Milton hardly ever spoke to each other without arguing. Producer Mike Todd, close to both Eddie and Milton, saw what was happening to them, but he would not interfere except to say to them both, "There is so much tension present, if you two don't come up with some kind of legal contract agreeable to both of you, you will end up killing each other!"

Eventually, they did come up with a legal contract defining their business relationship. On April 5, 1956, through New York attorneys, Mager and Mager, they formed RamRod Productions, Incorporated. It was intended to impersonalize their relationship. Each partner paid $12,500 for 100 shares of common stock. Each was to have all his services and money channeled through RamRod. Milton was president, and Eddie was secretary-treasurer.

Before now, no one has ever explained how they came up with

the name "RamRod." Milton's astrological sign of Aries qualified him as the "Ram," but one only conjectured what qualified Eddie to be the "Rod." In truth, there was a trumpet player from harlem who was one of Milton's clients. He and Eddie frequently waited together in Milton's office, hoping for job assignments. The term Ramrod in the harlem section of New York meant "Powerful." Therefore, when the musician would call Milton about a booking, he would say, "Hey, Ramrod. Do you have any jobs for me this week?"

Eddie found that amusing and on his first trip to California, he gave Milton a new Cadillac, bearing the word "Ramrod" boldly on the side.

Once when Eddie was appearing at the Tropicana, Milton was at The Desert Inn where he received a phone call saying Eddie had been in an automobile accident. Milton rushed over to find Eddie was fine, but Ramrod was demolished. Ramrod then became the unique name for their business partnership. As time passed, the friendship between the two men began to dwindle. The contract signed in hostility on April 5 had no real meaning within only a few years, even though they were supposedly bound to each other for the following ten years.

Milton attempted to maintain the friendship as well as the business relationship; but Eddie seemed to avoid Milton whenever he could. Mutual friends often found themselves in difficult and embarrassing positions, attempting not to take sides; Eddie seemed to enjoy finding people to spar against Milton with words. And although both men continued to visit Dr. Jacobson, each visited his office alone.

Shortly after Eddie and Milton had signed their contract forming RamRod, Grossinger's gave a testimonial dinner for Milton, to honor him for his years of service to the resort. Many celebrities, friends, and associates were there. But Eddie did not attend, conspicuous by his absence.

During 1956, Eddie's career continued to decline. Coca-Cola dropped his show *Coke Time,* and NBC paired him with George Gobel for a new television slot. He continued to record, but few of his singles made the charts, with only "Sayonara," "Cindy, Oh

Cindy," and "Around the World" doing well. And he continued to draw good audiences for his personal appearances, but the teenagers were not clamoring for him the way they had only three years before. They were clamoring for Elvis Presley. No matter, Eddie was still pulling in an enormous income; his agent, MCA, received $399,000 in commissions from him for the years 1956 through 1959.

However, Debbie's career was soaring to a peak. Her movie *Tammy* was an enormous success, and her recording of the title song reached number one on the charts, earning her a gold record that year. Whenever people asked Eddie if he was jealous of his wife's success, he responded with the insistence that he was very proud of Debbie's accomplishment.

After Debbie completed *Tammy,* RKO-Radio Studios scheduled a movie that would star Debbie and Eddie together. It may or may not have been something to do with the fact that Debbie was pregnant. It was entitled *Bundle of Joy**, and the stars, who were married in real life, were not married in the picture. The comedy was based upon their becoming the "parents" of a child by mistaken identity. Debbie was a sales clerk at a department store, and she became stuck with a foundling. Everyone assumed she was the mother; when the boss's son, played by Eddie, took an interest in her case, it was quickly assumed he was the father. It was innocent family fun, complete with six songs—but it bombed at the box office.

Debbie was seven months pregnant when they completed shooting on the picture. By careful diet and exercise, Debbie had managed to get through the filming without showing she was expecting. The baby, their first, was born on October 21, 1956, and they named her Carrie Francis Fisher. They were both delighted with their child. Debbie seemed to take naturally to motherhood, while Eddie was somewhat insecure as a father, possibly because he was still looking for a father figure to emulate. Milton had supplied that example for several years. Since they were no longer com-

---

* Bundle of Joy—All musical rights owned by Milton Blackstone Music Co. Formerly Blackstone Music, Inc., 221 W. 57th St., NY, NY 10019

municating, Eddie began to emulate his good friend, Mike Todd, the flamboyant theatrical entrepreneur, who had the self-confidence Eddie lacked. He even took up cigar smoking like Mike.

Although Debbie had someone to take care of the household chores, and a nurse to look after the baby, she took a break in her film career to spend some time being a mother. Eddie, however, had to keep working. When Carrie was seven weeks old, he and Debbie flew to Florida for an NBC convention, then to New York for the premiere of *Bundle of Joy,* and back to Los Angeles for the premiere there.

After only a year of marriage, the problems between Eddie and Debbie deepened into troubles. The second year, 1957, proved to be a critical one. Their differing work schedules prevented easy adjustment to each other; their divergent waking and sleeping patterns simply grew wider and wider. Eddie tried sleeping pills to counteract Jacobson's injections so he could sleep at night, but that only added to his drug dependency. Often Debbie would come home from a day's work to find Eddie and several of his friends or business associates sitting around the living room barechested, drinking and talking.

Finally, at Debbie's request, they both went to see a marriage counselor, who referred each of them to psychiatrists. Even that did not save the marriage.

In some ways, their close friendship with Mike Todd and Elizabeth Taylor helped; in other ways, it made things worse. The social life of married couples is often dependent upon the company of other married couples to maintain peace and harmony. It is difficult for single friends to be equally close to both husband and wife. When couples are friendly with couples, the men can pair off as friends, and so can the women. It makes a nice stable compromise. Sometimes.

Mike Todd had been a friend of Eddie's for a number of years. They first met through Milton Blackstone back in 1950. Mike was producing a revival of burlesque, called *Peep Show* at the Winter Garden Theater in New York, and Milton arranged for Eddie to audition for the show. He was not cast, but Mike remembered the young singer later when they met again.

Celebrated author Anita Loos has described Mike Todd as a "charming rogue, the kind of man for whom a beautiful woman would give the diamonds off her back and not ask why." He had no sense of shame or guilt or responsibility to anyone besides himself. He was suave and charming and self-confident, and people—both men and women—loved him. He was born Avram Goldbogen in Minneapolis; he never finished high school; and he began his career running lotteries, bookie joints, and strip shows. He graduated from con artist to successful Broadway producer without ever changing his techniques. All he needed was *chutzpah* and charm, and that was pretty much all he had. He could make a fortune overnight, and lose it just as quickly without ever blinking an eye or expressing regrets.

Eddie Fisher admired many of these characteristics, and he tried to acquire them, but it just didn't work. The "Papa's" shoes were just too big on the kid, but Eddie still tried to wear them.

Debbie had been friendly with Elizabeth Taylor when they were both under contract at MGM, but they had not been truly close friends. They became close when Mike began dating Elizabeth. The two couples were often a foursome; and, when Mike and Elizabeth were married on February 2, 1957, Eddie and Debbie were in the wedding, Eddie and Cantinflas standing as best men for Mike, and Debbie and Mara Taylor standing as Elizabeth's matron of honor.

Elizabeth was happy with Mike Todd. He could be extremely irresponsible; he would often ignore her, disappearing with the boys without even letting her know where he was going or when he would be back. But he was as good to her as he was bad. When he was with her, he gave her his undivided attention; and he was constantly giving her beautiful and expensive gifts.

Debbie was not so happy with her carbon copy of Mike. Eddie treated her with the same disrespect that Mike sometimes had toward Elizabeth, but Eddie had not acquired the other facet to Mike's personality. The irresponsibility was all that Debbie got.

In the spring of 1957, it seemed clear that the psychiatrists were not going to be able to save their marriage. They were already discussing separation when they flew to London for the opening of Mike Todd's *Around the World in 80 Days* on July 2.

They took a suite at the Dorchester Hotel, just a few floors below the Todds' suite. Eddie was in and out of the Todd suite frequently, while Debbie chose to remain in their suite alone. Mike was very big on gambling and playing poker. His poker games often went on all night; and, when Eddie wasn't playing, Mike would often send Eddie to check on Elizabeth. Eddie didn't particularly care for Elizabeth; he thought she acted like a spoiled child, making so many demands on Mike. But, because Mike had asked him, Eddie would go and sit with Elizabeth, talking mostly about Mike. When Eddie and Debbie were having troubles, they would also talk about Debbie. Eddie also talked to Mike about his problems with Debbie.

After the two couples went to the races at Epsom Downs together, Mike told a reporter, "All is not smooth at the Fishers. Eddie is a night-time boy. Debbie is a home girl."

If Debbie resented this public comment on her private life, she didn't show it. She and Eddie went on to stay with the Todds at their villa at Cap Ferrat in Southern France. However, when they returned to their new Holmby Hills home in California, they agreed to a separation with full intention of a divorce. Eddie was willing to give Debbie a one-million dollar settlement. The lawyers were drawing up the papers when Debbie discovered she was pregnant again. Eddie wanted to go ahead with the separation; but Debbie begged him to stay with her at least until the baby was born.

Eddie wasn't sure what to do. He called Milton Blackstone and asked for his advice. Milton, hoping this was a sign their rift was healing, advised Eddie to stay with Debbie. He was certain Eddie's fans would turn against him if he walked out on his wife while she was pregnant. So Eddie kept up the public pretense of being happily married.

In August, Elizabeth Taylor Todd gave birth to a baby girl by Caesarean section, and the proud parents sent the Fishers a family photograph—Mike, Elizabeth, and baby Liza. Eddie bought a sterling silver frame, and displayed the photograph in a prominent place in their living room.

On February 24, 1958, Debbie gave birth to a baby boy. They named their son Todd Emmanuel Fisher in honor of Mike Todd.

Todd was born just a few minutes before Eddie went on the air with his television show, and so the proud father was able to announce the birth to his 40 million viewers.

Only three weeks after Todd Emmanuel was born, Mike Todd was killed in the crash of his plane, the Lucky Liz. Elizabeth had been ill and did not accompany her husband on the trip.

As soon as Debbie received word of what had happened, she rushed to Elizabeth. Doctors had already arrived and given her sedatives, but the drugs had not been strong enough to put her to sleep. She was in a state of shock, refusing to believe that Mike was dead. To try to be of help, Debbie took Elizabeth's sons—Mike Jr. and Christopher—to her house.

Eddie was in North Carolina when he got the word, and he was stricken with shock, grief, and total bewilderment. He felt he ought to do something, but he did not know what to do. So he called Milton, who told him, "Go to Elizabeth. Comfort her."

Eddie flew home to California in time to accompany Elizabeth to Chicago for Mike's funeral. Debbie stayed at home to look after the children. While Eddie and Elizabeth had not been extremely close before, they now had a tie—their mutual grief for Mike.

The scene at the funeral was one Elizabeth was not accustomed to—a screaming mob. Eddie was used to screaming fans, but not at a funeral. Elizabeth during that nightmare was heavily sedated; Eddie was getting Jacobson's injections. The effect of the mob tearing at their clothes is incalculable. Certainly, for Eddie, he had experienced nothing like it since he had been the number one singing idol four years before.

Elizabeth remained in a state of shock for weeks afterward. She returned to her home on Coldwater Canyon in Beverly Hills and tried to come to grips with her loss. Because Mike's death was a loss to Eddie Fisher too, Elizabeth often called him to come over and keep her company. With Debbie's blessing, Eddie went. The two of them would just sit and talk for hours.

Mike had once advised Eddie to play Las Vegas. Eddie had believed that Vegas was not his kind of town, and he had avoided it. Now, however, he changed his mind and agreed to play the Tropicana that summer. Elizabeth decided to accompany Eddie and Debbie to Las Vegas; going to Eddie's opening with Debbie would be her first public appearance since Mike's death. Eddie was a success at the Tropicana, but Elizabeth got more attention, sitting at his ringside table listening appreciatively and smoking.

Eddie and Debbie had a fight over Eddie's gambling while they were in Las Vegas. He had become compulsive about it, and it may have had something to do with the fact that Mike Todd had been a big gambler. Mike had loved gambling more than anything, and he never cared if he lost big, because when he won, he won big. Eddie only lost big. With the help of his injections, he could gamble day and night without stopping. Debbie stood by his side through one night of losses, and then she left to go home to California.

As things deteriorated between Eddie and Debbie, they improved between Eddie and Milton Blackstone. After his opening at the Tropicana, Eddie called Milton and asked him to suggest the right words for a telegram he wanted to send to Elizabeth Taylor, thanking her for being there. Eddie, using his own name, sent Milton's words: "Your graciousness in coming to my opening is only exceeded by my gratitude."

Increasingly, rumors appeared in the gossip columns that all was not well in the Fisher household, but Eddie and Debbie continued to maintain the outward appearance of a happy couple. After his appearance in Las Vegas, Eddie was at home in Holmby Hills for a couple of weeks before he had to fly to New York on business involving his television show. Before he left, he and Debbie gave Louella Parsons an interview.

Before the columnist arrived, Eddie was at home alone with only the two children and the nurse. Debbie was out at a charity luncheon. He sat, the perfect image of the proud father, playing with Carrie while the nurse looked after Todd. Carrie was just beginning to speak words now; she was becoming like a real little person, and Eddie could better relate to her. It may have been that he had a premonition of what would be happening in the next few weeks, but he was gripped with an overwhelming sadness. He gave Carrie to the nurse and decided to take a dip in the pool before Louella arrived.

He was his usual affable self when he sat down to talk to

Louella; and, when Debbie came home, she joined them sitting by Eddie and holding his hand like the happy, contented wife. By the time the sweet, domestic interview appeared in the fan magazine, Eddie's and Debbie's marriage had ended.

Debbie took Eddie to the airport to see him off on his flight to New York. He had given her the day and time of his return flight; Debbie agreed to meet him at the airport.

When that flight arrived, Debbie was at the airport, but Eddie was not on it. He would not be coming home at all.

10. Triangles

The 1950s were drawing to a close in an atmosphere of schizophrenia. Social commentators were talking about the "Silent Generation," young people in their twenties who selfishly sought their own material goals while denying any social responsibility. In terms of age, this was also the "Beat Generation," but the two groups were opposite poles of the same social and cultural phenomenon. The "Silents" sought home and family and security; the "Beats" denied themselves all that, turning inward, and wandering about the country "enjoying the moment." The Silents would grow old into the "Silent Majority," and together they and the Beats would produce the "hippies" and the "flower children."

If the public remained silent and secluded, snug in the comfort of security or freedom, the public press did not. Television had become the number one medium of communications, and its self-concept was that it was to "entertain" and to "inform." It saw nothing schizophrenic about that self-concept; in truth, weren't they one and the same? With the immediacy of television, news needed to be more sensational than thought-provoking. And because of the success of television news, the livelihood of newspaper and magazine writers became threatened if they could not be more sensational than their visible counterparts. Rapidly, the public right to know became the public right to pry.

There was a lot happening in America and in the world in the fall of 1958—presidential advisor Sherman Adams had to resign because of improper use of official influence; Chinese communists were bombarding Matsu and Quemoy; the U.S. was successfully aiming rockets toward the moon and ballistics missiles as far as

6,000 miles; the U.S. and the U.S.S.R. were negotiating a limitation of nuclear weapons; airlines were scheduling the first transatlantic jet flights. But gossip and rumors about Eddie Fisher and Elizabeth Taylor, often took precedence over these matters.

The atmosphere of schizophrenia appeared most blatantly in the public's attitude toward its mythological figures—its gods and goddesses. The deities of sex and love had been held sacredly separate. As a part of the silence of the times, sex had become severely repressed, and at the same time it had become an obsession. In the wake of Joseph McCarthy, a great many politicians and news columnists had set themselves up as guardians of the public morality, under the assumption that the American people were less responsible and less mature than they were.

Much of the mythology of love and sex in the twentieth century had been created by the Hollywood Movie Studios; and, for more than thirty years, they had controlled what people read about their gods and goddesses. Not only was this good business and public relations, guarding the properties and investments they had, but it also permitted the deities a certain amount of privacy or even secrecy in their time away from the public eye. Often the private person was nothing like the public god, but that didn't matter. However, in the late 1950s, the Hollywood Studios were fading, losing their power and control, soon to go out of business completely. As much as they might try, they could no longer protect their deities from public prying.

It took many more years before newspeople and public were able to accept stars of the entertainment world as people rather than gods and goddesses. Because these deities symbolized love or sex, the motive behind their every action—in the public mind—had to be love or sex; they could not have a full human dimension of emotions, thoughts, doubts, fears, anxieties, weaknesses.

Elizabeth Taylor was so very beautiful, the public could not imagine that she had anything on her mind but sex. Eddie Fisher and Debbie Reynolds looked so sweet and innocent, they couldn't possibly involve themselves in anything except their pure love for each other. The mythologies about these three people were nothing whatsoever like their real and private selves. The great misfortune for all of them was that the sexual frustration of the public (represented by the newspeople) was reaching the breaking point by 1958. Eddie Fisher, Debbie Reynolds, and Elizabeth Taylor were to be sacrificial lambs in the triumph of sex over love, so that—in the years that followed—the American public could be free of love to revel in unrestrained sex.

At the time, sex—as represented by Elizabeth Taylor—was the villain, luring faithful husband away from true love. Only later was it possible to look back and see that she was not at fault at all; in fact, that none of the three principals was at fault. The real villain was the script written by the public and by the news media.

Malleable Eddie Fisher had been pushed into marriage with Debbie Reynolds by the public. He was now being pushed out of that marriage and into one with Elizabeth Taylor in the same way.

It was Eddie's 29th birthday and Elizabeth had asked him to stop by her home so she could give him a present—something that had belonged to Mike.

Their feelings for each other had already been aroused several times before while they had been in the company of friends, but this time, they were alone and their feelings were more intense.

Eddie recalls entering her house . . . "Elizabeth's eyes. I can't ever forget how they burned into my heart that day. I felt her need for me from the depths of her soul. My feelings were identical to hers." This was the beginning of a romance that shocked and revolted a nation, if not the world.

Eddie was scheduled to go to New York on recording business. When Debbie drove him to the Los Angeles airport, she had no idea that he would be running into Elizabeth Taylor in New York. As far as she knew, Elizabeth was on her way to Europe in hopes of escaping the prying crowds that clamored at her wherever she went in the United States. However, Elizabeth had been detained in New York by red tape: she could not travel on her passport because it was a joint passport for Mr. and Mrs. Michael Todd. She had to apply for a new one for Elizabeth Taylor Todd.

Shortly after arriving in New York and checking into the Essex House, Eddie met with a few friends. Elizabeth Taylor was among the group, and she was registered just down the street at the Plaza

Hotel. They were good friends, and to those around them, there seemed to be no reason why they should not be seeing each other. They went out for dinner and drinks a number of times, but rarely were they alone together. Most of the time they were accompanied by Elizabeth's agent friend, Danny Welkes.

One evening they went to dinner and afterward stopped in at the Blue Angel with Eva Marie Saint. The press agent for the Blue Angel hurriedly telephoned columnist Earl Wilson. Minutes later, Wilson arrived to take a photograph. When Eddie saw the camera, he ducked. The gossip columnist assumed this action connoted a guilty feeling, and so began the story of a romance between Eddie and Elizabeth.

However, one item in a column does not a romance make. Everyone involved could easily ignore one small suggestion. But once the seed was planted, it was inevitable that it would blossom. A few nights later, Eddie and Elizabeth were at The Embers having drinks and talking. Eddie mentioned that he had to go up to Grossinger's the next day to help dedicate a new swimming pool. Elizabeth mentioned that Jennie Grossinger had invited her to come up as well, but she hadn't decided whether to go or not. Would it look funny if they went up together?

Eddie didn't know, but he could call Milton at Grossinger's and get his advice. Milton's response was, "If she wants to come, bring her along. There'll be a big group here. We'll wait for you."

They all stayed in Harry Grossinger's cottage. Elizabeth had her own room, Milton had a room, and Eddie and Danny Welkes shared a room.

Elizabeth's decision to accompany Eddie had been so sudden that she had been unable to pack some clothes to take along. They were going to be there only for the weekend, and Eddie suggested they could just as easily pick up a few things at Grossinger's. Elizabeth went to Stephen's Resort Shop in the hotel and picked out three swimsuits, two pairs of slacks, four blouses, and three sweaters, charging them to the Blackstone Agency. Milton picked up the tab.

Elizabeth Taylor came back to life that Labor Day weekend almost six months after the death of her husband. She was able to laugh again; more importantly, she was able to force herself to look at pictures of Mike Todd and think of the happiness they had shared. Now she was enjoying herself with Eddie Fisher, who had loved Mike almost as much as she had.

Eddie, who was supposed to return to Los Angeles to spend his third wedding anniversary with Debbie, decided to stay with Elizabeth. In turn, Elizabeth, who was supposed to leave for Europe to escape for awhile at the house she had rented at Antibes, decided to stay and spend more time with Eddie.

The two of them really had no plans, and it might have all turned out to be nothing more than a pleasant interlude if it hadn't been for two things. The first was that newsmen happened to note that Eddie and Elizabeth seemed to be at Grossinger's together, and not just there to dedicate a swimming pool. The other was that Eddie decided now was the time to tell Debbie he was ready for the divorce they had been talking about. Yet, when Debbie placed several telephone calls to him, he refused to accept the calls.

She still hoped that Eddie might "reform" and that their marriage might be saved. When the first items began appearing in the gossip columns, Debbie decided to take the offensive. On September 9, she chose to make a public statement of shock and dismay at the stories of a romance between her husband and Elizabeth. "What's wrong," she asked, "with a friend taking a friend out in the evening?"

However, Eddie flew home to Los Angeles the next day to get things straight between him and Debbie. He wanted her to know quite clearly that he wanted out of their marriage. The following day, September 11, Debbie's studio, MGM, issued the statement that Eddie and Debbie were to be legally separated. Promptly, Eddie moved in with his old friend Joey Forman, and Debbie slipped off to stay with her friends Marge and Gower Champion until the initial hullaballoo passed over. Elizabeth flew home to Los Angeles to be near the children. Naturally the press assumed she was flying to be with Eddie. The days and weeks that followed were like a circus; newsmen were everywhere that Liz or Eddie or Debbie appeared, asking the same questions, constantly armed with innuendos. It hardly mattered whether or not the public wanted all of the gory details; the newsmen were creating a sensation, and they wanted as much as they could get. Unfortunately, in trying to defend themselves, all three of the principals gave the newsmen what they wanted. Elizabeth was the sexy and sophisticated seductress; Eddie was the slave to his own helpless passions; and Debbie was the injured innocent.

Whether it was at the prodding of MGM, or a need to protect her own interests, or just plain hurt and anguish at the injury, Debbie did more to maintain that picture of the situation than did Elizabeth or Eddie. Debbie persisted in giving the impression that her marriage had been happy until Elizabeth came along. That was, of course, untrue. Some people in recent years have commented on the fact that Debbie is not so sweet and innocent, that she is in reality tough and demanding, implying that she never was the wholesome All-American girl she appeared to be. But a woman in her forties who has endured in show business for thirty years would either have to be stupid or a fool to remain innocent all that time. When she first met Eddie Fisher, Debbie was sweet and innocent; she toughened up a bit after living with him for two years.

Unintentionally, Elizabeth added some fuel to the flames. She made the terrible mistake of trusting Hedda Hopper, whom she had been close to since she had been a child. The famous columnist had often given her motherly advice, and she had also kept confidences Elizabeth had shared with her. Elizabeth needed someone to confide in, and she chose to talk to Hedda Hopper.

Elizabeth was honest and forthright in what she said—that Eddie was not in love with Debbie, that they had been planning a divorce, and that she (Elizabeth) could not take something away from Debbie that Debbie never really had. But she touched off Hedda Hopper's sense of moral outrage, and Hedda printed (selectively) what Elizabeth had told her in confidence. It came out as proof that Elizabeth was just what everyone thought she was—a selfish temptress.

In reality, Elizabeth had a good head on her shoulders; she was both sensitive and sensible. In any other circumstances she probably would have realized that Eddie was not the right sort of man for her. But she desperately missed Mike Todd; and, in many ways, she could see Mike in Eddie. If she had had perspective then, she might have realized that, although Eddie was in love with her, she did not love Eddie. She still loved Mike, and she was simply transferring some of that love to his carbon copy.

As for Eddie himself, it is to his credit that he honestly and earnestly tried to impress upon the public that the whole thing was his fault. He tried to explain that his marriage to Debbie had failed long before this. However, he would not yet admit to the public—nor to himself—that probably one of the major reasons his marriage had failed was his addiction to drugs. If he had been able to realize in 1958 that the erratic life-style brought about by the drugs was not conducive to lasting relationships, he might possibly have been able to pull himself away from them and been able to save himself. But drugs do not have a tendency to give an addict much perspective.

On December 4, 1958, Debbie filed for a divorce before a perturbed judge who remarked, "If Fisher's publicity is only one-tenth truthful, this divorce is a disgrace." On February 19, 1959, she received her interlocutory decree and property settlement of one million dollars plus child support. The divorce would be final in a few months. Carrie and Todd Fisher would see very little of their father in growing up; the responsibility of rearing them would be entirely Debbie's. In fact, the Fisher children would see very little of the Fisher family. Surprisingly, the one member of Eddie's family who took the greatest interest in them was the father Eddie feels never gave him much attention—Joseph Fisher.

The bad publicity hurt the careers of all three of the principals, perhaps hurting Debbie least of all. Her career continued to go well for some time, flagging slightly in the late Sixties, when cutesiness had gotten too old to be interesting or appealing. Elizabeth Taylor, having given one of the finest performances of her career in *Cat On A Hot Tin Roof,* was nominated for an Oscar but failed to get it, largely because of the publicity. Eddie's career was hurt most of all. Already flagging, it now almost completely disappeared. On January 6, 1959, he was notified by NBC that his television show was cancelled, and so was his contract with them. Sales of his recordings had dropped to the point of being invisible, so there was not much of a calling for new songs. Eddie was able, however, to continue some of his nightclub appearances, and Elizabeth courageously helped him by appearing ringside as a special added attraction for the public's morbid curiosity, but that was not until they were able to announce their engagement publicly.

In March of 1959, Elizabeth officially changed her faith to unite herself with the Jewish religion. Naturally everyone assumed it was a part of her preparation to marry Eddie Fisher. However, she had considered doing it for some time; her marriage to Mike had decided it.

Elizabeth stood solemnly before the Ark of the Covenant and the Holy Scrolls and answered the ritual questions from Rabbi Max Nussbaum: "Do you promise to cast your lot with the people of Israel amid all circumstances and conditions? Do you agree to rear your children according to the Jewish faith?"

Then she gave the pledge: "I, of my own free will, seek the fellowship of Israel. I believe that God is one, almighty, all wise and most holy. I promise that I shall endeavor to live, as far as in my power, in accordance with the ideals of Jewish life. Most fervently, therefore, do I herewith pronounce the Jewish confession of faith: *Schma yisroel adonoy elohena adonoy echod. Boruch shem Kuod malchuso l'olom voed.* (Hear, O Israel: the Lord our God, the Lord is one. Praised be his name whose glorious kingdom is for ever and ever.)"

She took as her Jewish vowels, Elisheba Rachel.

Eddie was growing impatient for his divorce decree to come through so he and Elizabeth could be married. He tried to get Debbie to agree to a quickie Nevada divorce, but she refused. Finally, he decided to announce the engagement before his divorce was final.

On April 1, 1959, on Debbie's twenty-sixth birthday, Eddie opened a six-week engagement at the Tropicana in Las Vegas. Elizabeth attended the opening; and, at the party afterward, she displayed a diamond bracelet that was her engagement gift from Eddie. Eddie announced that they intended to be married before his engagement at the Tropicana was over. He was taking up residence in Nevada, he said, and would get a quickie divorce.

They were married in Las Vegas on May 12, 1959, the day Eddie's Nevada divorce was final. Elizabeth was dressed in a moss-green chiffon cocktail-length dress, and she carried a bouquet of yellow and green orchids. They said their vows under a perfumed canopy of carnations, orchids, and gardenias at the Temple Beth Sholom, while police held back the crowds outside. Mike Todd, Jr., and Milton Blackstone were Eddie's attendants. Elizabeth's sister-in-law, Mara Taylor was her matron-of-honor. Rabbi Max Nussbaum conducted the wedding ceremony.

As the happy couple left the Temple, they were met with loud boos and shouts from the crowd. By now they were accustomed to the public abuse.

On his wedding day, Eddie had barely a dime in his pockets; Milton had to give him a thousand dollars so he would have some cash for his honeymoon. Unlike Debbie, Elizabeth got a lengthy honeymoon away from all the crowds. But, then, everything about Eddie's marriage to Elizabeth was different from his marriage to Debbie.

Elizabeth believed the only way Hollywood marriages could succeed was for the married couple to work together. When Eddie had an appearance, Elizabeth would be there and a part of it; when Elizabeth had a picture, she would like it if Eddie would do the picture as well. If Eddie were not to be in the picture, he would have to try to arrange his schedule so that they would never be away from each other for more than a day. After Mike's death, this sort of attitude toward being separated became almost an obsession.

Unfortunately for Eddie, this attitude meant the end of what little career he had left. He was little more than Elizabeth Taylor's caretaker for the next three years. Elizabeth did not want it that way; that is simply the way it turned out.

For their honeymoon, Eddie and Elizabeth flew to Spain where they picked up the yacht *Olnico* loaned to them by movie producer Sam Spiegel; then they took a long cruise off the Mediterranean. After that, Eddie went with his wife to Spain and England while she made the film of Tennessee Williams's *Suddenly Last Summer*. Then it was back home to the United States.

In late September, Eddie and Elizabeth attended the Fox luncheon for visiting premier Nikita Khrushchev. They were mortified, as were most of the American people, at the rude treatment given the Russian premier by the Fox executives and the Los Angeles mayor. Eddie and Elizabeth later attempted to make up for this international *faux pas* by hosting a party for the visiting Moiseyev Dancers. Married to Elizabeth, with her wide interests, Eddie found Milton had been right years ago in advising him to read *The New York Times.* He now had some catching up to do.

After the Fox luncheon, Elizabeth accompanied Eddie to Las Vegas for his appearance at the Desert Inn. Eddie had accepted the fact he was no longer a "teenage idol" and made attempts to alter his style for a more mature audience. For the Desert Inn appearance, he brought in Colin Romoff, a New York voice coach and song stylist to supervise the musical aspects of the show; and actor-director Mel Ferrer staged the program. But the big draw was to be Mrs. Eddie Fisher—Elizabeth Taylor.

Opening night, the place was packed with an excited and enthusiastic crowd. When one couple at a ringside table was asked which of the Fishers they had come to see, they had responded immediately, "Are you kidding? Liz—who else?"

Promptly at 11:45 P.M., Elizabeth made her entrance, beautiful in a white gown that set off her dark hair and violet eyes. She moved languidly to her place down front and center. Sitting elegantly, she put a cigarette in its long holder and chatted with Tony Curtis and Janet Leigh.

When Eddie appeared (after the show girls and the comic), he sang better than he had for a long time. By the third song, "Never on Sunday," sung in Greek, he had the audience with him. As the crowd cheered, Elizabeth glowed proudly. As she glowed, the flashbulbs popped. Despite how well Eddie was doing onstage, she was still the star of the show—offstage.

Eddie realized this, and he began to sing the songs directly to her—"Tonight," and "It Happens Every Spring." However, he had planned the ending very carefully. He gave the impression he had finished singing, and he spoke to the audience, remarking, "I opened here two years ago. Since then nothing much has happened to me." The audience roared with laughter. He then went on to

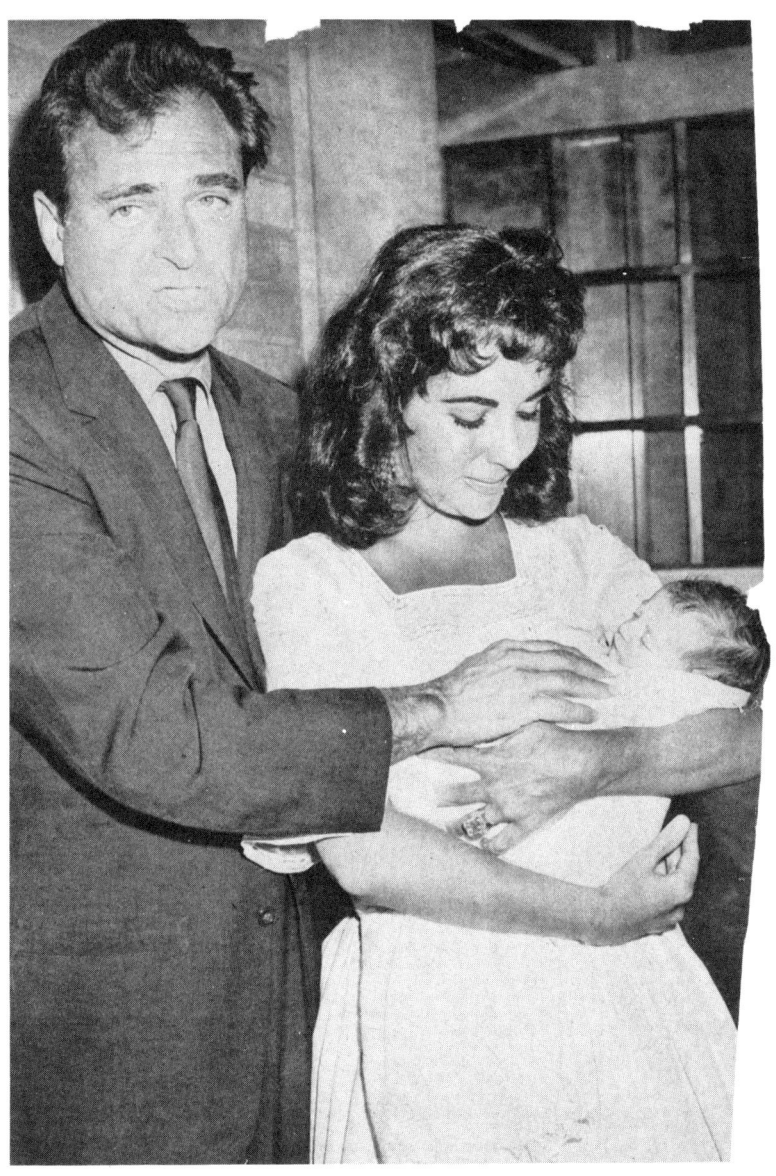
Mike Todd, Elizabeth and baby Liza.

Eddie and Elizabeth.

thank all of the people who had helped him with the show, and to introduce the celebrities present. Finally, he concluded, "Well, that's all. I think I've introduced everybody."

Naturally the audience realized he had failed to introduce his wife. "No, no," the yells came from all over the room. "What about Liz?"

With a look of mock surprise, he looked down at her table warmly and lovingly, and the audience hushed. "I'm so proud. And I feel so lucky that she's here tonight. But I think you how how I feel. Ladies and gentlemen, I'd like to present—Mrs. Eddie Fisher."

The audience cheered and whistled. Elizabeth waved to the crowd and blew Eddie a kiss. Then Eddie gave his planned ending to the show. He sang "That Face" directly to his wife—"Those eyes, those lips, that fabulous smile . . ."

This was to be the way they would work together, helping each other as one. So far it was working, and they knew exactly what they were doing. They also had fun doing it.

On Eddie's closing night, Elizabeth decided to play a trick on her husband. She disguised herself as a waitress, and moved about the room while Eddie performed. The audience could recognize her, but Eddie could not. When Eddie sang out the last high note of his final song, Elizabeth dropped a tray of dishes to the floor. The audience roared with laughter, and Eddie was dumbfounded until he realized who the waitress was.

In order to get out of her 20th Century Fox contract, Elizabeth found she had to do one last film for them; as it turned out, it would have to be a film she very much did not want to do—*Butterfield 8*. However, in October, she finally agreed to do it. Following their plan to work together, Fox also signed Eddie Fisher for a part in the picture.

Their marriage was supposed to be a 50-50 arrangement, but rapidly, Elizabeth became the dominant partner, carrying Eddie Fisher along, at least as far as the public could see.

On November 29, 1959, Eddie was to open an engagement at the Empire Room of New York's Waldorf Astoria Hotel. The press was not overly excited about the event; they weren't particularly interested in interviewing Eddie Fisher; however, his wife was another matter. With Elizabeth's approval, Milton Blackstone arranged a party for the midnight show, inviting 72 celebrities to be Eddie and Elizabeth's guests for the ocassion. There was a strict seating arrangement, with tins of caviar and with champagne and assorted other beverages for the six reserved tables; Elizabeth to pick up the tab of $1,500 for the night.

However, there was a problem. A party of fifteen, headed by a Brooklyn dentist, had seen the first show and was not willing to give up the tables needed for Elizabeth and her guests to sit together.

As Elizabeth entered, glittering with diamonds, a hush went over the crowd. She approached the table where the dentist sat, and asked them courteously to leave.

The party refused to budge. They fully intended to sit through the second show. As the stalemate persisted, Elizabeth's temper flared, and so did the dentist's. Rudely, he announced to the still standing Elizabeth, who was nervously twisting Mike Todd's 29½-carat engagement ring, "Listen, lady, we knew Eddie when he was just a waiter at Grossinger's, and our money is as good as yours!"

That remark gave Elizabeth her solution; she called the waiter over, paid the squatters' $500 check, and then demanded, 'Goddam it, get your asses out of here."

The suspense in the room was growing as the lights dimmed and the musicians took their places. Finally, the group left, and Elizabeth and her guests were able to be seated. The tension, however, had reached Eddie backstage. He was not at his best for his opening night. His performance was not bad, but neither was it his best.

When the two-week engagement at the Waldorf ended, it was the last time Eddie Fisher sang publicly for a year and a half. And the problems began for Eddie and Elizabeth—not marital problems, but health problems, particularly Elizabeth's health. While Eddie was still at the Waldorf, Elizabeth went into the hospital with pneumonia.

In January they began filming *Butterfield 8* together in New

York, and the first big problem with their plan to do everything together became evident: Eddie Fisher just was not an actor, nor did it seem likely he could learn to act. He came off completely flat and stiff onscreen.

The wounds between Eddie and Milton Blackstone seemed to be completely healed by now, probably because Eddie desperately needed Milton's help. Money was coming in through RamRod, and Eddie needed every penny he could get. Even though NBC had cancelled Eddie's contract, they were obligated to pay $100,000 a year to RamRod. Eddie was getting some money from his nightclub appearances, but there had not been a great many of them. For *Butterfield 8,* Ramrod was paid $100,000.

Eddie still had to pay $40,000 a year in child support for Carrie and Todd. His half of RamRod did not now amount to a great deal. And the expenses to Dr. Jacobson continued to mount for both Eddie and Milton.

On Sunday, January 10, 1960, Milton gave Jennie Grossinger a testimonial dinner at the Hotel Astor in New York. All proceeds were to go to launch a drive to build the Jennie Grossinger Medical Center in Israel. Over 1,500 people were there to pay tribute to Jennie, including a great many celebrities—Joey Bishop, Red Buttons, Elaine May, Buddy Hackett, Dr. Max Jacobson, Freddie Robbins, and Elizabeth Taylor and Eddie Fisher. Eddie Cantor was chairman of the affair, with Eddie Fisher, Paul Grossinger, and Milton Blackstone serving as co-chairmen.

For Eddie and Milton, it was a fitting end to the decade of the Fifties. The Sixties would not treat either of them as well.

The 1960s began with a ray of hope; the young people who were products of the wartime baby boom were coming of age; and, just as their parents had fought a war to make a better world, they were determined to rid that world of injustice and repression and prejudice. "Peaceful and non-violent protest" was the keyword of those who were attempting to end racial segregation in the South. And a new, young politician named John F. Kennedy would endeavor to offer America a "New Frontier" in which the people would again participate in their government.

Alas, the promises were cut short; and the decade of the Sixties proved to be one of chaos, confusion, tragedy and despair— the inevitable legacy of the Fifties.

And Eddie Fisher, so much a part of the Fifties, inherited his share of the legacy. For him, and for Elizabeth Taylor, the Sixties began with an epic catastrophe known as *Cleopatra,* and another romantic triangle. Elizabeth had been offered the title role in the film back in October of 1959. She didn't like costume epics, and didn't quite know how to turn the producers down. She was the top box office attraction in the country, having been nominated for three successive years for the Oscar, the latest nomination being for *Suddenly Last Summer.* Eddie recommended to her that she could easily get out of doing the picture by making impossible demands—an unheard of one million dollars against a percentage, full script control, and selection of much of the production personnel. To their astonishment, and to the astonishment of the public, the producers agreed to all of Elizabeth's demands. The contracts were finally signed in July of 1960; shooting was to begin in September.

Because of their determination to be together and to work together, Elizabeth had Eddie contracted to look after her and insure that she would be able to work on schedule; he would be paid $1,500 a week for that service. With all the best intentions, they had planted the seed that would destroy their marriage.

In August, they took a cruise in the Greek Islands to rest before shooting on *Cleopatra* would begin. In September, they arrived in London for filming, taking the Penthouse at the Dorchester Hotel. Promptly Elizabeth fell prey to the first of a long series of illnesses. For the rest of the year, she was in and out of the London Clinic for everything from a virus to an abscessed tooth to meningism. The film company shot around her as long as they could, but finally had to shut down indefinitely in January of 1961. Except for one quick trip home in October, Eddie was at Elizabeth's side constantly.

She recovered and was able to do some shooting on *Cleopatra* in January; but, from all appearances, it was headed for disaster. They were already seven million dollars in the hole; they had little footage of the star; and all the scripts were so bad, they had to be junked. Elizabeth asked to be released, but the producers refused. Shooting stopped again in February; and Elizabeth and Eddie flew to Munich, Germany, to begin arrangements to adopt a little German girl named Maria Heisig.

The girl had parents, but she had also been born with a defective hip, and the Heisigs were unable to pay for the kind of operation and continued medical care that Maria would need to lead a normal life. The parents had put her up for adoption hoping a wealthy couple could give the child a better chance at life.

Since Liza had been born, Elizabeth had been unable to have another child of her own; she and Eddie wanted children, so adoption was their solution. (Eddie also officially adopted Liza Todd, and he and Elizabeth also asked her former husband Michael Wilding to allow Eddie to adopt his children, but Wilding refused.)

On February 16, the Fishers had to rush back to London so that Eddie could undergo an emergency appendectomy in the London Clinic. Then Elizabeth again became ill, this time with the Asian flu, which became complicated with pneumonia. Elizabeth was allergic to ordinary antibiotics; but, without them, she grew worse daily.

On March 4, Eddie discovered that his wife was unconscious and unable to breathe. He called the hotel desk, and they were able to locate a doctor in the building. After trying everything he could to help Elizabeth to breath, the doctor informed Eddie that her only chance to live was with a tracheotomy, a hole cut into the throat so that a tube could be inserted. It would, he impressed upon Eddie, leave a scar.

Eddie instantly made the decision; anything to save his wife's life. It was probably the fastest decision that the normally indecisive singer ever made.

But the worst was yet to come. Elizabeth was taken to the London Clinic, where she hovered between life and death for days. Fans set up a vigil outside the hospital. As the woman who had been called the "most beautiful woman in the world" hovered near death, all was forgiven her. As much as everyone had hated her before, everyone loved her now. Even Eddie was forgiven. All over the world, people kept vigil; the Soviet Union officially notified the doctors that a government plane would be at their service to fly in any drugs that might be necessary.

On March 6, Eddie was told that his wife's condition was hopeless, that there was no way they could save her, that she would die. She was in a coma, and her leg was badly affected from the drugs they had given to her. Eddie pleaded with them to tell him if there was anything at all that might save her. There was a drug, they informed him, but it was not available in England. There was only a slight chance that it would help, and they ordered it from the United States, but it was being shipped by mail. It would probably not arrive in time.

Eddie called Milton Blackstone in New York. "I'm going to lose her," he told him. "She has to have a certain serum because she's allergic to antibiotics." Then he pleaded, "Please help me to help her to live. Please. I love her so much. If she dies, I'll die."

Milton responded quickly, "Don't give up hope. Give me time to see what I can do. Call me in about an hour."

Milton immediately called Dr. Jacobson, whom Eddie had already called. Milton learned the necessary medicine was Staphage Lysate, a product developed by the Lincoln Foundation at Delmont Laboratories in Swarthmore, Pennsylvania. He arranged to have it delivered to Dr. Jacobson's office.

Milton then made a reservation for the next flight to London, arranging to bypass customs by having a hospital car waiting for him at the London airport. The arrangement was to be: if the car was there, Elizabeth was still alive; if not, Milton was too late.

When he arrived, the car was waiting to rush him to the London Clinic. He waited with Eddie for the outcome. By March 9, the crisis was past. Eddie stayed awake around the clock, and he spent almost all of his time at Elizabeth's bedside. Everytime she gained consciousness, however briefly, Eddie was there. Later Elizabeth described the experience of regaining consciousness: "I saw Eddie. He had been there every time I became conscious, encouraging me to fight for my life and telling me I was improving, even though he knew I wasn't. I felt an overwhelming sense of love for him."

In the days and weeks that followed, Elizabeth had to have Eddie by her side constantly. When he had to be away from her, even for a short while, she would grow anxious and have him paged—either as "Mr. Edwin Jack Fisher" or "Mr. Sonny Boy Fisher." Wherever he happened to be, whenever he heard the page, he would rush to her side.

Eddie's love for Elizabeth was so great that he transformed his habits completely. He still depended upon the drugs to keep going, but he was no longer the irresponsible, carefree, carousing Eddie. He was devoted to his wife, and he became her constant attendant, serving her, waiting upon her, devoting his every moment to her. He did not realize it, nor did Elizabeth yet see it, but he was losing his individuality, becoming Mister Elizabeth Taylor, the very thing that the public had been accusing him of being.

At the end of March, Elizabeth was well enough to leave London, though not well enough to resume shooting on *Cleopatra.* They returned to Los Angeles on March 28 to rest at home.

By April 18, Elizabeth was feeling well enough to attend the Academy Awards Ceremony, although her leg was still bad and Eddie had to help her to walk. She was nominated for the Best Actress Oscar for the fourth consecutive year, but she did not expect to get it, because it was for *Butterfield 8,* the worst of all her recent films. When her name was announced, she was shocked. She threw her hands up to her face and looked at Eddie. He nodded in confirmation, and helped her walk up to the stage to accept the award. She knew, as everyone else did, that it had been given her by way of an apology for the way the movie industry had mistreated her in preceding years.

Cleopatra would not begin shooting again until September, a full year after the original filming was supposed to have begun. Meanwhile, Elizabeth and Eddie were free. They gave parties for the visiting Russian Moiseyev Dance Troupe, and they attended the Moscow Film Festival in July, returning to Los Angeles afterward so that Elizabeth could have plastic surgery done on her tracheotomy scar.

Also in that July of 1961, Eddie was to make his first singing appearance since the Waldorf appearance of 1959. It was at the Cocoanut Grove in the Ambassador Hotel in Beverly Hills, and it was a charity performance, with funds to go to Eddie Cantor's Surprise

Lake Camp. The audience was almost entirely made up of celebrities, and Eddie Fisher had a bad case of stage fright: since he had not appeared in so long, people would take special note of his appearance, his voice, and his style to see what his years offstage had done to him.

The evening was a disaster, primarily because of Frank Sinatra and friends. Eddie's troubles that evening began with a faulty microphone, but Dean Martin, Sammy Davis, Jr., Jerry Lewis, George Jessel, and Frank Sinatra were not sympathetic. After two songs that were barely audible, Eddie went into the third. That was when the heckling started.

Eddie stopped singing and pleaded, "How about letting me finish the song?"

Dean Martin snapped back, "Hell, you haven't finished the others yet."

Eddie held his temper and tried to continue as gracefully as he could, but the heckling increased. Elizabeth, who was sitting in her usual place down front, was fuming. When Eddie went into his final song, "That Face," sung to Elizabeth, Dean Martin let go with the clincher:

"And that's some face there. I don't know why you're working. If my wife had that face, I'd be home working with her."

When he had finished the song, Eddie attempted to make it all appear to be good-natured kidding. He walked to the Sinatra table, addressed the group as the "Desert Mafia," and made a wisecrack about their invading Cuba. However, they were not to be outdone; they took Eddie back on stage to "show him how it's done," clowned around, and cracked obscene jokes, to the mortification of the star-studded audience.

That evening finished off whatever dignity was left to the singing career of Eddie Fisher. Within a few months, his dignity would receive further blows; and these would come from the most unexpected source of all, from his beloved wife.

What had begun in a triangle was to end in a triangle.

The filming of *Cleopatra* had been moved from London to Rome, and the shooting was to resume for Elizabeth in September.

She and Eddie took the children and all their dogs and rented a house, the Villa Pappa, at an expense of $2,880 a month beginning September 1. Their staff consisted of a nanny for the children, a butler, three menservants, four maids, two chauffeurs, a kitchen boy, a chef, a laundry woman, and a woman to do the ironing.

Their life in Rome resembled a circus, aided and abetted by the Italian *Paparazzi,* those photographers who go to any extreme to get unusual and saleable photos of celebrities—the more outrageous the better. (One actually punched Elizabeth in the stomach to get a very startled picture of her.) Some of the *paparrazi* swore that, if Elizabeth did not have a romance with another man during her stay in Rome, they would create one for her.

As it turned out, they didn't have to.

Elizabeth had a rugged schedule of filming; she had to get up and into costume and makeup well before sunrise. Therefore, she had to be in bed no later than nine in the evening. It was essential to a film production that was already well over budget; and Eddie had been put on salary to see that his wife adhered to that schedule. Considering Eddie's irregular sleeping habits, it was a strange thing to do. However, it may have been intended to make Eddie himself feel responsible so as not to tempt Elizabeth into going along with his tendencies.

It worked too well, to the extent that Eddie became Elizabeth's jailer, and she grew to resent that. When Eddie had been irresponsible and unpredictable, he had been fun. Although Elizabeth did not like the listless and morose Eddie she saw when his drugs had worn off, the energetic Eddie on the injections was as wild and as free as Elizabeth herself was.

Maintaining a social life with that schedule was difficult, but Eddie and Elizabeth attempted to go out on the town or to entertain at home as often as they could. A frequent companion on these evenings was the actor playing Mark Anthony in the film— Richard Burton.

Burton, a Welsh Scorpio, was notorious for his amorous adventures. He was also noted for his arrogance, his irreverence, his carousing, his long-winded stories, and his whimsical pranks. He was, in short, a charming rogue, exactly the kind of man who would appeal to Elizabeth. The more Eddie tried to keep Elizabeth to her schedule, the more Richard Burton tried to lure her away from it.

Elizabeth delighted in being lured. It quickly became a game between her and Burton as to how to thwart her jailer-husband's schedule.

By the middle of December 1961, the game had turned the relationship of Eddie and Elizabeth into one of animosity. Elizabeth had begun to yell at Eddie and to put him down almost continually. And the more Eddie tried to remain the dutiful and loving husband, the worse the situation became.

11. The Fallen Idol

By January of 1962, the marriage between Elizabeth Taylor and Eddie Fisher was over, but Eddie didn't know it yet. Elizabeth had him barred from the *Cleopatra* set because, in the love-scenes, she could not help but show how she was beginning to feel about Richard Burton. If Eddie suspected what was happening, he did not show it. In fact, it was a relief to him that suddenly Elizabeth was no longer demanding that he be by her side. Since that change, Eddie had been too occupied with thoughts of his career to notice what was happening to his wife.

After almost two years of waiting upon Elizabeth hand and foot, Eddie had some regrets about having given up his career. During the preceding year, Elizabeth had experienced one illness after another, and she had been insecure about Eddie leaving her side. Now that she was well and fully occupied in making *Cleopatra,* she did not need him constantly by her side. Eddie took this opportunity to return to New York for a while to get his career going again. He needed to talk to Milton Blackstone, to try to set up recording sessions again, to see if he could get nightclub appearances, and do some guest appearances on television. If the public had forgiven Elizabeth, surely they had forgiven him as well.

While he was in New York, the gossip began about Elizabeth and Burton, but Eddie was accustomed to the rumor-mongering of the news media, and he ignored it. In February, however, Eddie received the report that Elizabeth was in the hospital again; immediately, he rushed to Rome to be by her side. Something was different now; he was kept waiting for hours outside her hospital room. And when he was permitted in, he was permitted to remain only a short time. He had learned the truth.

But he was not going to accept it. He would use the same tactics to keep Elizabeth that Debbie had used to keep him. He was going to give the outward appearance of a happy marriage, hoping Elizabeth would come to her senses and give up her lover. On February 27, Eddie gave his wife an elaborate birthday party and presented her with an expensive diamond ring as a birthday gift. But pretense would not work any better for him than it had for Debbie.

Eddie appeared on the *Cleopatra* set unannounced to see for himself what was going on. And he saw. "It wouldn't have mattered if I had sent them an engraved announcement telling them the time I was arriving," he remarked later. "I'm sure he was as helpless as I had been. They couldn't keep their eyes, not to mention their hands, off each other."

The ties of marriage seemed to mean nothing to the lovers. Burton walked up to Eddie and announced, "I think you should know I'm in love with your girl."

Eddie responded, "Well, she's not your girl. She's my wife."

To which Burton countered, "Well, I'm in love with her, so get out of here."

Eddie just stood there, helpless and dumbfounded, and angrier than he had ever been. He contemplated violence, but he knew if he slugged Burton the sympathy of the press would turn from him to the lovers. Eddie also had a gun which he threatened to use on Burton. Luckily, Milton convinced him to leave Rome and return to New York.

Milton Blackstone was deeply concerned about Eddie's state of mind. Eddie alternated between rage and disbelief; kept up by Dr. Jacobson's injections, he was not fully in control of his thoughts and actions. Afraid that Eddie might do something rash, Milton persuaded him to go into Gracie Square Hospital in New York for a rest. The reports in the newspapers that Eddie was in a special "psychiatric ward" were untrue, but efforts were being made to stabilize his attitude toward the affair. In fairness to Dr. Jacobson, it should be noted that Eddie probably couldn't have survived this period in his life had it not been for the doctor's treatment.

When Eddie came out of the hospital, he called a press conference at the Hotel Pierre, issuing a statement that there was nothing to the story of an affair between his wife and Burton. To prove it, he gambled on calling Elizabeth by telephone to confirm his story to the reporters. Elizabeth refused.

To prove to her husband that their marriage was over, Elizabeth sent a committee to call upon Eddie at the Hotel Pierre on April 3, 1962. The committee consisted of Elizabeth's business manager Kurt Frings, Mike Todd Jr., and Mike's accountant. They were there to convince Eddie that his wife wanted a divorce, and that his cooperation would be the only reasonable solution. They succeeded in convincing Eddie that Elizabeth was serious about a divorce; however, they did not succeed in convincing him that he should be cooperative.

He had given up everything for Elizabeth. He had agreed to give his first wife a settlement that was more than he could really afford at a time when his career was going downhill. He had spent what little he had left on his new wife, much of it on extravagances. And he had completely given up working to be by her side. He was now broke and faced with beginning a career all over again at age thirty-four. He was not about to make things easy for his wife.

The seemingly deepest problem for Eddie at this time was his excessive dependency upon Dr. Jacobson's injections. They were growing less effective, and so he needed them more often. He had begun to question if they really were good for him. But, if he brought up the subject with Milton Blackstone, Milton—a regular Jacobson patient—would defend Jacobson. When Eddie questioned Jacobson himself, the doctor insisted they were not harmful. To prove it, he took Eddie with him to the White House while he gave president John F. Kennedy injections. (JFK liked to quiz Eddie about his love life, but Jackie Kennedy thought Eddie was a complete bore.) As long as Eddie had Jacobson's constant care, he would be all right. But Eddie worried about the day he might not be able to afford the expensive treatment.

His total personality became reversed, even to the point where he could no longer successfully hide his harbored feelings of animosity toward his parents and especially his brother, Bunny

(Alvin), who once had aspirations of also becoming a singer. Eddie resented this and would do nothing to help him succeed, causing the brothers to be worlds apart.

Bunny is a tall, slender fellow with an out-going and friendly personality; he openly idolized Eddie. Many times when Bunny (as well as other family members) tried to telephone Eddie, he would be conveniently "out."

The spring and summer of 1962 was a very difficult time for Eddie. He did not want to face reality, but he knew he had to. Everything had fallen apart, and he had to try to pick up the pieces. Frank Sinatra offered Eddie his Palm Springs home to escape for awhile, and Eddie took him up on it, while Milton Blackstone went about trying to get Eddie's career going again.

That spring, Eddie made his first record in some time; it was "Arrivederci Roma," recorded for RCA. Milton figured they ought to try to capitalize on the scandal. However, he warned Eddie, "The first thing you will probably be asked is, 'Why did you ever record a song like this after all that has happened to you? " He told Eddie that his reply should be, "What did you expect me to sing, 'Take Me Out to the Ball Game'?"

Milton advised Eddie not to ignore what was happening in the press. If there were danger of an audience laughing at him, then he must get to the laugh one step ahead of them.

Eddie also had to start dating other women to give the impression he was no longer mooning over Elizabeth, which he was indeed doing. Eddie picked the youngest and most beautiful women he could find. Ann-Margaret was his most frequent companion, but he also dated Renata Boeck and Stephanie Powers.

Milton had not lost his magic touch. He quickly began to set up a full schedule of nightclub appearances for Eddie—Las Vegas, Lake Tahoe, the Cocoanut Grove, appearances in Chicago and Philadelphia, his old standby Grossinger's, and the Latin Casino in New Jersey. The most exciting appearance of all was to be a special show at the Winter Garden Theater in New York.

But something happened to Milton Blackstone in June of 1962 that affected all those around him, even Eddie Fisher and Jennie Grossinger. Milton had always devoted his life to his work and to others. He had looked after his mother, and he had always been there when clients such as Eddie or Jennie needed him. Now, at age 56, he decided to get married, and he found what it was like to be torn between private life and public obligation. At a time when all of his money and effort were going toward rebuilding the career of Eddie Fisher, he discovered a wife restricted his freedom somewhat.

Monte Proser and Milton Blackstone were producing *Eddie Fisher at the Winter Garden,* with Juliet Prowse and Dick Gregory, to open in October of 1962. To do this, Proser and Blackstone had to put up $75,000 each, out of their own pockets.

On opening night at the Winter Garden, Monte Proser was stricken with a heart attack. Dr. Jacobson was present backstage to give Eddie an injection, and he rushed to Proser's side prepared to give him one. Harvey Mann, production co-ordinator of the show, stepped in, saying, "What are you trying to do, kill him?" Monte recovered without the injection.

Eddie performed very well at the Winter Garden, but the engagement proved to be a disaster because of a couple of skits that Juliet Prowse insisted on keeping in the show. One was a Cleopatra routine, with specific references to Elizabeth Taylor and Richard Burton. It was supposed to be funny, but the audience didn't laugh. No one, not even Eddie, could persuade her to take the skit out. Most people who saw the show noticed the enormous change in Eddie; he was no longer the sweet-faced young kid. In fact, he looked older than his 34 years. The wear and tear of drugs and a hectic life were showing in the lines and wrinkles already appearing on his face. Only his voice remained the same.

When Eddie was at the Winter Garden, he received a call from Frank Sinatra, asking Eddie for a favor. Sinatra had ownership in a club at Lake Tahoe. He wanted Eddie to perform there. Grateful to Sinatra for the help he had recently given to him, Eddie immediately said yes.

Milton was furious; he had made other plans for Eddie. "Don't go," he pleaded. "You'll ruin everything."

Las Vegas was not the place for Eddie to be in his present unhappy condition. Mike Todd had taught Eddie the joys of gambling, one of which was to lose yourself completely in the game. During this engagement in Vegas, gambling became such an escape to Eddie that he quickly began to lose more than he had and more than he was earning. Immediately after his act, Eddie would head straight for the tables; anyone in his way, except for his female companion of the evening, would get an instant brush-off. During just one evening, he lost $250,000.

Milton tried to reason with him, but that didn't work. Eddie responded, "You gamble; why can't I?" Milton then tried to speak to the club owners, asking that they not permit Eddie to lose more than $5,000 at a time. But, when Eddie found out, he became furious at the club owner and at Milton, and he simply moved on to another casino.

The vicious circle of drugs now was accompanied by another vicious circle—losing money at gambling and then having to borrow money to cover those losses and to live. Eddie had to borrow $32,000 to pay his income taxes. As long as Milton could get the money, he passed it on to Eddie, always expecting it back. But lenders were quickly running out.

Soon Eddie found himself playing engagements to pay off his gambling debts. The situation became desperate for him during 1963. When he tried to get Milton to borrow another $100,000, it was the beginning of the end of their relationship. Milton refused to get him more money until the $32,000 was repaid.

Eddie had begun to surround himself with a new set of friends, and they had been trying to separate Eddie from his dependence on Milton. They felt Milton would not let Eddie grow up, and they were certain they could handle Eddie's career better than Milton had been doing. With Eddie now in a rage because Milton wouldn't throw more money his way, his friends were able to persuade Eddie to try to get rid of Milton. Together they approached Milton with a demand he sell Eddie his half of RamRod.

Milton was hurt and bewildered. "Eddie," he asked, "why didn't you come to me by yourself? Why this way?"

Eddie's response was curt: "Oh, hell, be realistic. There is nothing more you can do for me. I can take care of myself and handle my own business affairs."

They spent six hours in a restaurant discussing Eddie's proposal. Finally, Milton made an offer, "If you pay off the debt you already owe, I'll settle for $250,000—or $25,000 a year for ten years." Eddie agreed; however, at that time, he didn't have the money, so the sale never went through.

Eddie's friends felt they could work around that little problem. A few days after their discussion, Eddie and Milton were on a plane to Ohio, where Eddie had agreed to substitute for Jennie Grossinger at a fund-raising benefit for Wilberforce College. Milton picked up a copy of *Variety*. On the front page was a story reporting that Eddie had bought and paid for Milton's stock in RamRod. Milton was indignant, but Eddie insisted that he had not planted the story.

On November 7 Leonard Lyons reported in his column, "Eddie Fisher and Milton Blackstone no longer are client and manager. In their new set-up they'll be 'associates.' Fisher said: 'This means I'll ask his advice more often.' "

The relationship did continue much as before, but Eddie continued to bring up the subject of buying Milton out of RamRod. On November 22, the day John F. Kennedy was assassinated, they were again having lunch, trying to come to some working arrangement that would be satisfactory to both of them. Tragedy apart, the negotiations bogged down.

The divorce between Eddie and Elizabeth had also bogged down in wrangling over money. Spokesmen for Elizabeth announced publicly that Eddie was responsible for the delay because he was asking for an impossible settlement of one million dollars from her. He countered by announcing that what he wanted was $750,000 tax free, plus the use of $250,000 over the next ten years. (Presumably that quarter of a million was to be used to buy out Milton's share of RamRod.) He emphasized that this amount was not a settlement from his wife, not a handout: "The nature of the dispute is not my request for money, it is the determination of our mutual property." (Do these sound like Eddie's words or Milton's?)

In December of 1963, Sybil Burton finally got her divorce from Richard; and suddenly Eddie seemed to be standing in the way of his wife's happiness. Burton and Elizabeth were in Mexico filming *The Night of the Iguana,* so she filed for a Mexican divorce. On March 5, 1964—after two years of separation—Elizabeth received her divorce decree from Judge Arcadio Estrada in Puerto Vallarta, on the grounds of abandonment. On those grounds, Eddie could not ask for any settlement.

Eddie's response was to lead a wilder life, if indeed that was possible—more gambling, more drugs, and more women. He was seen with different women more than ever before.

The year 1964 was a time of strained relationships for Eddie Fisher. In the disputes between Eddie and Milton, Dr. Max Jacobson, close friend to both, often found himself having to take sides, one against the other, which only compounded their problems.

Milton was losing his magic touch; the treatment had begun to affect him so severely that he was having difficulty performing his work effectively. Because of their close friendship, Jacobson continued to care for Milton.

Though Eddie once claimed to trust Dr. Jacobson totally, and even to love him, he now seemed to want to prove to every one that he no longer needed him. He could get his drugs from someone else. A man who had been an employee of Jacobson's in New York had now separated himself from the doctor, and he was illegally supplying drugs to big name stars in California.

According to Eddie, after an extreme bout with anxiety in 1966, the physician wanted to give him a needle in the stomach. Eddie panicked and decided to break off all relations with Dr. Jacobson, turning to his new supplier for his needed drugs.

By that time, most people were becoming aware of the full effects of all the drugs that had been introduced in the 1950s—the tranquilizers, the sleeping pills, the amphetamines. They and harder drugs were increasingly becoming available on the streets, and some people were beginning to talk about a "drug problem" among the young.

While Eddie Fisher was going through a period of personal rage and personal despair, the entire country was feeling rage and despair on a broader level. The non-violence of the early civil rights demonstrations had proved to be an amazing success; but, after the death of President Kennedy, demonstrators increasingly provoked violence or turned to violence themselves.

Rock and Roll music had graduated from Elvis Presley to the Beatles' pure "Rock" sound; and it in turn was giving way to something called "Hard Rock," something the older generation would call "noise."

The American nation was beginning to get tangled up in a civil war in Vietnam, very much the way it had become entangled in Korea, but this one would prove to be even more insoluble than the "police action" of the 1950s. This one would last for years and eventually split the American nation in half. And resistance to it among the young provoked even greater violence than the civil rights movement had met.

In 1964 and 1965, Eddie Fisher was not greatly aware of the outrage and despair going on around him. He had much too much of it to deal with in his own life. He spent much of 1965 playing engagements to pay off debts. He continued to bicker and argue with Milton until finally they arrived at a permanent parting of the ways.

But not before a very embarrassing incident occurred in Miami, Florida. In February, Eddie was playing the Fontainbleau Hotel. Milton and his wife happened to be in Miami with Jennie Grossinger. Milton's wife and Jennie wanted to go to Eddie's opening. Milton and Eddie weren't speaking so Milton didn't notify him they would be there. When Eddie came on to sing, he noticed Milton in the audience and became flustered and infuriated. Backstage, Eddie let out a few choice words about Milton's presence, and he later accused Milton of being present just to embarrass him.

At this point in his life, Milton was not capable of anything so calculating. The medication was now affecting him so severely that his mind and his speech wandered. At times Milton talked so irrationally no one could understand him. The man who had once been so suave and quick-witted now often gave the appearance of being feeble.

Milton could not see the change that had taken place in himself; it was as though he were the spectator and the man he saw was the participator. Friends were astounded by the transformation in him after an injection. He would talk continually, with no one able to get a word in edgewise. He seemed to be full of physical strength and vigor. But as soon as the medication wore off, he would be like a dying man, shaking from head to toe, then becoming withdrawn, going into black depressions.

It had become obvious to Eddie Fisher that he could not buy his way out of RamRod; and now when it seemed Milton was not fit either physically or financially to stop him, Eddie formed his own company, Future Productions.

Milton, who had become so engrossed in trying to straighten out Eddie's tangled life, didn't foresee or recognize the problems erupting in his own personal life. Never having had a marriage built on deep affection, Milton more or less allowed his wife to come and go as she pleased, making life as comfortable for her as possible, including an exclusive apartment in Florida and a home at the Plaza. Sometimes she would stay at her home in Woodmere while he lived in their New York apartment.

In 1965, she went on a vacation in Switzerland. She had been informed about a doctor there who could increase longevity and youthfulness; she wanted to visit him.

Milton made arrangements for her trip and called people he knew in Switzerland to tell them of her coming so she would not have to continually be among strangers. Driving her to the airport, he expected to see her in the near future.

But in a few weeks he received a long distance telephone call from his spouse. She told him not to meet her at the airport when she arrived back in New York, for as far as she was concerned, the marriage was over.

As his step-daughter was staying with him at Grossinger's, Milton had the responsibility to inform her of the marriage break-up. He had always felt his marriage was somewhat like a computerized match, programmed for a two-year period until his step-daughter would become of age. The divorce was not contested and quickly was resolved.

Events in Milton's life reached a climax through an unpleasant episode at Grossinger's. As Jennie had gotten older, her health had grown steadily worse. Her son, Paul, now a responsible adult, was professionally schooled in hotel management and operation. As a protegé of Milton's, he had his own ideas about how to run Grossinger's. Finally, a situation arose whereby Paul and Milton had conflicting ideas as to a possible solution to a problem. Paul asserted himself by saying, "No!" to Milton's proposal.

Milton did not want Jennie ever to be placed in a situation where she would have to choose between her friendship to him and loyalty to her son. He therefore decided the time had come to quietly make the break with Grossinger's, which he did.

Very quickly, Milton ran out of money, and he no longer had income from any of his businesses. The IRS and accountants took action to obtain what finances he still had left in reserve. Yet, Dr. Jacobson continued to treat him. And because he was a friend then, Milton has never allowed an unkind word to be said about the doctor in his presence.

Milton's brother, Leo Schwartzstein, approached everyone who knew Milton, asking them please not to try to help him because the family would see that his needs were met. He made one condition to Milton—that he discontinue seeing Dr. Jacobson. Milton refused.

Daniel Blackstone also made efforts to help but Milton balked at this. "Don't interfere," he would tell both brothers.

Milton quickly learned that when your money is gone, so is your liberty. People who knew him didn't even recognize him as he walked the streets of New York looking shabby and seeking a handout. He sought shelter in hotel lobbies and service quarters as personal dignity became annihilated; he existed more and more in his withdrawn, recluse world.

Hearing what had happened to Milton did not cause Eddie to seek help for himself. Nor did it cause him to offer help to the man who helped him become Eddie Fisher—Star. Instead, he began to mix his drugs, and he began to mix them with alcohol as well.

Publicly, he became typed as a "loser," but Eddie Fisher was not really a loser, not by the technical definition. One psychologist has noted, "Losers find a perverse pleasure in being unhappy," but Eddie derived no enjoyment in sharing his problems with the public. Having broken away from Milton, Eddie was earnestly trying to make a comeback. He had, in 1965, managed to play a great many lucrative engagements—from the Desert Inn in Las Vegas to the Palace Theater in New York. But all of the money was going toward paying off his enormous gambling debts. And what he made was still insufficient for that because he could not help but keep gambling.

12. Ups and Downs With Uppers and Downers

Eddie had no intention ever of marrying again. The routines of marriage simply did not fit in with the kind of schedule his career and personal habits necessitated. He seems to have been entirely satisfied with brief romances and one-night stands after his separation from Elizabeth. If he didn't get too deeply involved with a woman, he could easily dump her when and if she got in the way.

His attitude was not a callous one; it had become common among the young people of the mid- and late 1960s. Love was no longer a viable relationship between two people; it was something one wore on a lapel button or scrawled on walls with spray paint, and it was something one could only feel for all humanity. Sex was the deeply personal relationship, and one sought as many personal relationships as one could get. Marriage as an institution, a formalizing of a personal relationship, was on its way out.

In the late 1960s, sex and nudity were proclaimed as a great new breakthrough in the theater and motion pictures. It was a piece of drama, to enjoy watching as much as to enjoy participating in. Broadway shows such as *Hair* and *Oh, Calcutta* and movies like *Last Tango In Paris* brought sex out of the bedroom and into the eyes and minds of millions.

The public-private life of Eddie Fisher had done much to free American audiences of restraints. It was only natural that he should reap the benefits as much as anyone else.

When Eddie met a bubbly young blonde actress and singer named Connie Stevens, he expected only another brief romance.

Certainly, he never expected to fall in love.

Connie was appearing on Broadway in a Neil Simon comedy entitled *The Star Spangled Girl*. She was already well-known from her role as Cricket on television's *Hawaiian Eye*, and from her hit recording of "16 Reasons." She had recently been divorced from actor James Stacy.

Half Irish and half Italian, Connie was a Catholic; and, despite the fact her first marriage had not worked out, she still had the old-fashioned attitudes toward the sanctity of marriage. When and if she fell in love with a man, she fully expected the final result to be holy matrimony.

Eddie was honest with her from the outset. "Baby," he suggested after their first meeting, "let's do our thing but not fall in love."

"Okay," Connie responded, "I'll try not to if you try not to."

Eddie was also honest about what sort of life he led, "I'm a man of many vices. I'm a compulsive gambler, I like to drink, even though I haven't been drunk in years, and I don't buy sex but I crave the love of a woman."

Their relationship began free and flexible, very much according to the philosophy expressed by the song Eddie recorded that year, "Games that Lovers Play." It was to be a relationship with no rules except for the one Eddie had set up: "Don't get serious."

With Connie's background, it is likely that she never had any intention of following that rule. But Eddie himself also found it impossible to follow as well. However, even after he told friends, "I'm in love; I thought I would never feel this way again," he was still determined not to take that terrible step to marriage again.

Connie began writing tender love notes to Eddie just to remind him how much she cared. Fearing he was being unfaithful to her, she flew to wherever he was appearing, even if only to spend a few hours with him. It quickly became apparent that Connie wanted more than just Eddie's love; she wanted his name as well. Finally, she issued an ultimatum: "If you're not prepared to marry me now, then start looking for another girl."

Despairingly, Eddie asked, "How much more do you want from me?"

"Everything," Connie answered, "that's what loving means." Eddie had a few choice words for his response. He also had a problem: he loved Connie, and he did not want to lose her. But he simply did not want to marry her. Even if he did want to marry her, there was another complication: Eddie was still attempting to contest Elizabeth's Mexican divorce; he was not willing to let go of property he felt was legally his. If he married Connie, he would be acknowledging the validity of his divorce.

After lengthy consideration, Eddie came up with a compromise. He and Connie would become engaged, but they would not set any definite wedding date. He bought Connie an engagement ring with a five-carat marquise diamond, and they announced their indefinite engagement.

He also took her to Philadelphia to meet his family. Connie and Eddie's mom got along very well. This time, Eddie's mom prayed, let it last. While they were in Philadelphia, Eddie and Connie appeared on the *Mike Douglas Show,* and Connie described how Eddie had given her the ring. She explained how she had been sleeping on the sofa in her apartment before leaving for the theater to do her show when Eddie quietly slipped into the room and placed the ring on her finger. She described it as being all very romantic, but she knew very well he had not offered her a wedding date, and that he might never offer her one.

It did not occur to Eddie that Connie might become pregnant. During her marriage to James Stacy, Connie had suffered three miscarriages, and doctors had given her little hope of ever having children. In January of 1967, Connie informed Eddie she was pregnant, and the doctor had given her a thirty percent chance of delivering. She would pass the danger point in April. After that point, she would have to let the public know she was expecting. Would Eddie marry her? Eddie said "no."

In April, after her pregnancy became common knowledge, and gossip columnists were buzzing, Eddie decided to say "no" publicly. He was still carrying on his legal battle with Elizabeth, and he was not about to have Connie interfere. He was appearing at the Waldorf Astoria in New York at the time, and he issued a public statement that he had no intention of marrying Connie Stevens, concluding with, "If she wants to have my baby, that's fine with me."

He did, however, borrow $9,000 from a night spot owner to pay for the doctor and the hospital. The amount was to be repaid in personal appearances. It never was.

On April 25, 1967, Eddie went on tour doing a two-man show with comedian Buddy Hackett, starting at Detroit's Fisher Theater (where they grossed $81,000 for eight performances), and going on to Philadelphia, Baltimore, Pittsburgh, St. Louis, Cleveland, Chicago, Toronto, Washington, and San Francisco. Connie gave up her role in *Star Spangled Girl* to accompany Eddie.

On June 25, Eddie and Buddy opened their two-man show in New York. Buddy Hackett did his routine to much laughter and applause. When Eddie came onstage, he was feeling pretty high, and he also felt the need to top what had preceded him, so he turned the speakers up. The sound was unbearable, prompting the audience to get up and walk out, asking for their money back.

He did not get the kind of press he needed at this point in his career. The public was beginning to get the impression Eddie was childish and egotistical; his audiences seemed unwilling to forgive him.

Eddie must have sensed some of this. He had to have good publicity soon or his career would continue to slide. He realized his obstinate refusal to marry Connie had hurt her severely. She was serious about her Catholic religion; having her baby illegitimately and continuing to live openly with Eddie faced her with possible excommunication from her church, unable to receive its sacraments.

When Connie gave birth to a baby girl on October 29, 1967, at St. Joseph's Hospital in Burbank, California, Eddie decided they would announce they had been married secretly—even though they had not. Eddie was in Las Vegas at the time, playing the Frontier Hotel; he arranged for his public relations man, Joseph Halperin, to make the announcement. Connie signed the hospital forms as "Mrs. Eddie Fisher."

They decided to name the baby "Joely," Al Jolson's nickname.

The marriage between Eddie Fisher and Connie Stevens was not

Eddie and Connie.

"Some" of Eddie's women.

Barbara Hayman
Elizabeth Taylor
Debbie Reynolds
Connie Stevens

Joan Wynn
Terry Richard

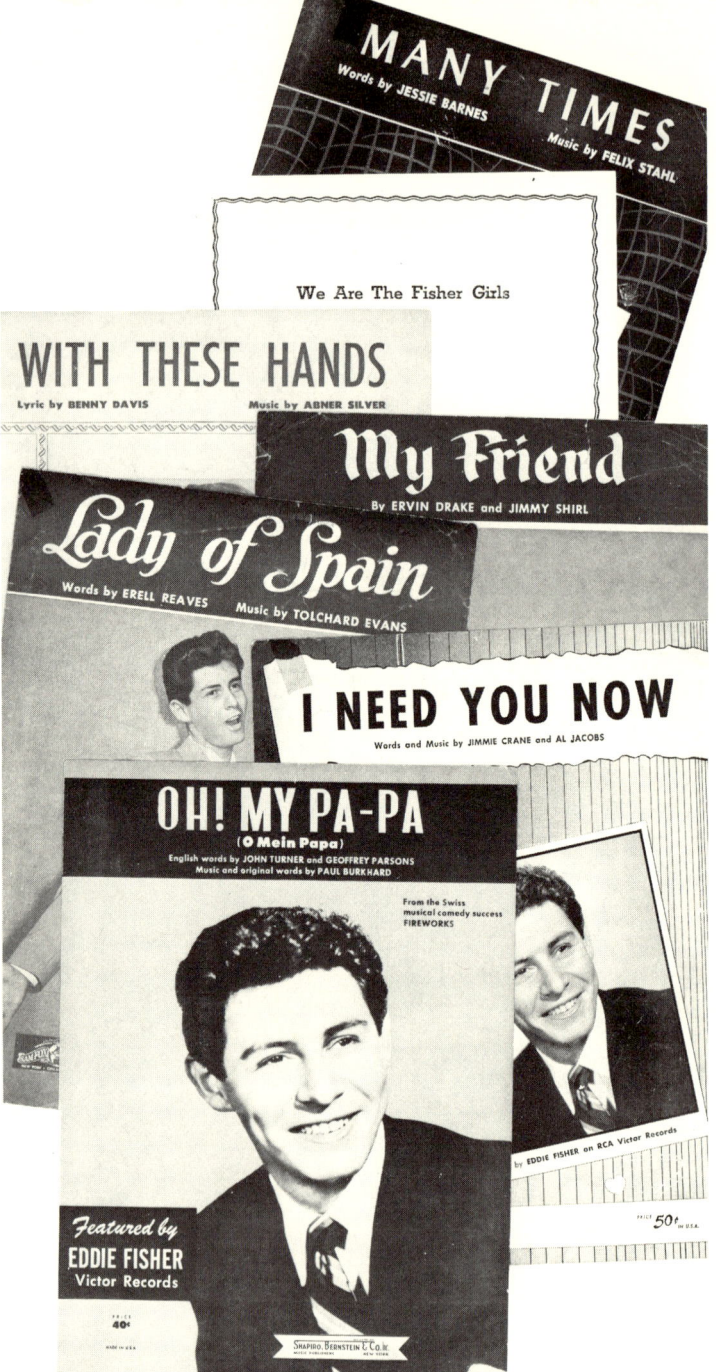

Some Eddie Fisher hits.

Fisher children with their mothers.

Carrie, Todd, Joely and Tricia.

Mrs. Daniel Blackstone with Debbie after performance of "Irene."

Daniel Blackstone, Milton's faithful brother.

to take place until February of 1968, although Eddie, Connie, and Joely lived as a family, giving the public the impression all was legal. The actual marriage, then, had to be kept secret; it was performed while Eddie was appearing at the Fontainebleau in Miami, Florida. Frank Sinatra happened to be there making a motion picture, and he lent the couple the use of his private Lear Jet so they could fly to San Juan, Puerto Rico, and get married without anyone's knowing it.

Eddie said later, "It never should have taken place at all. Anywhere." He was probably right; because, once the marriage had taken place, the fights began.

Connie and the baby moved into Eddie's small house in the Los Angeles area. Babies had never had a great appeal for Eddie until after they were past the wetting and crying stages and had developed their own personalities. He felt hemmed in, tied down. And besides, when he was not working, he had a tendency to let himself go completely with the drugs.

Their first big fight took place in March, on a Thursday evening, just over a month after their marriage. It went on all night and into the next morning. Finally, Connie couldn't take it any longer. She had the nurse pack up Joely's things, and they moved out of the house and into a motel in Sherman Oaks. If her move was a threat, Eddie didn't seem to mind; he went out to a discotheque called The Factory that evening with a group of friends. Connie moved back into the house on Saturday.

After that, things seemed to go well for awhile—at least on the surface. Eddie was about to become a producer, and he had every intention of working at it. With his singing career floundering, he envisioned a whole new career for himself behind the scenes. He owned the film rights to the big Broadway hit musical, *Paint Your Wagon;* Milton had had the foresight to buy those rights for Eddie years before, intending that Eddie would star in the picture. Now Eddie had made a deal with Paramount Pictures to make the film with him as Executive Producer. Alan Jay Lerner, who had written the lyrics to the show's musical score, would be Producer.

In mid-April, Eddie reported to Paramount's Melrose lot to be assigned his office by Paramount Executive Bob Evans. When Eddie discovered his quarters were much inferior to those of Producer Alan Jay Lerner, he was furious; he was certain that Bob Evans was getting even with him for stealing his girl back in 1963. He did not report to the Studio again. He left home every morning, telling Connie he was going to work; instead, he went to the home of a friend who had once worked for Dr. Max Jacobson. The house, in Beverly Hills, was private, expensive, and supplied with every convenience—executive secretary, valet, pool, and drugs. It was a perfect place for Eddie Fisher to hide out from his wife, and from the world.

With the help of various drugs, Eddie attempted to give the appearance of regular habits. Connie was much opposed to the drugs Eddie was taking, and she was trying to encourage him to kick the habit. What Eddie was doing was taking uppers to get through the day, and downers to be able to sleep at night.

In May of 1968, the vicious circle of uppers and downers began to catch up with him. One morning, Connie had to leave the house before Eddie was out of bed. He tried to get up shortly after that, but he was groggy from the pills he had taken to sleep the night before. The housekeeper had prepared breakfast for him, and Eddie went to the dining room to eat—or, more accurately, to try to eat, because he was swaying in his chair so badly he could get no food to his mouth. When Eddie passed out, falling off his chair onto the floor, the housekeeper and baby nurse became extremely upset. They tried to rouse him, but they had no luck. They called his doctor, who insisted he be rushed to the hospital. That proved to be unnecessary, but when Eddie was finally revived, he begged everyone not to tell Connie. However, Connie found out, and she was furious.

During this time, Eddie was trying to put together an entirely new act to open at the Frontier in Las Vegas on June 11. Earnestly trying to change his image, he had recorded some new singles and albums directed toward an older and more sophisticated audience. His single, "People Like You," had done well so he recorded an album by the same title. And he was recording an album entitled "You Ain't Heard Nothing Yet" paying tribute to Jolson by doing all Jolson songs.

Ups and Downs with Uppers and Downers 173

For the new act, Eddie had hired songwriter, Jules Styne, and all of the songs would be new to Eddie. He would do none of his own standards. The new Eddie Fisher would be a suave, sophisticated man-of-the world. His clothes would be flashier, more "Mod," with brightly colored shirts open at the neck and big heavy rimmed glasses.

Jules Styne came from New York to give Eddie the new material and to give him his ideas on the act in May; then he went back East, leaving Eddie to learn the material before Styne returned to California on June 6, only a few days before the opening.

When Styne returned, Eddie still had not memorized the lyrics to the new songs. They worked frantically for four days trying to get Eddie ready to appear. When Eddie still could not remember the lyrics on the day of the opening, they decided to give him a music stand to read from.

Opening night at the Frontier was an absolute disaster. Eddie barely managed to get through the early show by reading from his music stand. During his break, he was deeply upset and depressed. When he went on for the midnight show, he was unable even to get through the first song. After stumbling around with the lyrics for a few moments, he suddenly broke off and walked offstage. No one could convince him to go back on, and they had to bring down the curtain. The patrons walked out and demanded their money back.

On the Strip, the word was out about Eddie Fisher, and it was all bad. The Frontier was owned by Howard Hughes, and the Hughes executives had to call a meeting to decide what to do about Eddie's contract; they wanted to be fair to Eddie, but they could not have patrons walking out every night. After lengthy discussion, they decided to let him continue by going back to doing all his old standards to avoid slip-ups.

While Eddie was attempting to learn the new act, Connie gave him a video tape recorder so he could film his rehearsals and then look them over critically to see what he might need to change. Eddie, however, found another use for it; he had been seeing a great deal of a number of young women. He discovered taping some of them on the VTR could be fun.

Although Eddie was not doing very well onstage, he was having a terrific time off. Connie had not been able to come to Vegas for his opening, and she could pay only occasional visits to him, commuting from Los Angeles. So Eddie considered himself free to entertain any or all of his friends in his hotel suite or his dressing room. Eddie had always had people hanging around, even from the beginning of his career. There had always been a party going on; the only difference was that now the parties were getting a bit wilder. The "friends" who hung around now were continually changing.

His Beverly Hills friends came to spend time with him frequently while he was playing the Frontier, usually bringing female companions for Eddie. Steven Brandt, of the Brandt theater chain, also into drugs, was often there as well, and he too supplied female company for his friend. (After the Sharon Tate murder, Brandt was terrified about the discovery he had been supplying the actress with drugs, and he committed suicide). Guy Marks, the comedian appearing with Eddie, was often around as well.

When Connie paid an unexpected visit to her husband and discovered what was going on, she was furious. She was particularly upset that Brandt was with him, because she had told Eddie before that she never wanted them to be associated. Eddie was just as furious at Connie for being so possessive. After she returned to Los Angeles, Eddie was still simmering; to show her he would not be "tied" to her, he gave the gold wedding band Connie had given him to a comic friend. Several days later when the comedian visited the Fisher home, Connie ordered him out.

In July, soon after Eddie closed at the Frontier, Connie opened her act at the Flamingo in Las Vegas. Eddie was back in Los Angeles preparing for his appearance at the Cocoanut Grove in August, but he did come down for Connie's opening. It was then she informed him she was expecting another baby.

In his better moments, Eddie was aware that much of what his wife was attempting to do was actually for his betterment. He knew the drugs were harming him; but he was unable to do anything about them. He had to have them. One thing Connie had managed to accomplish with Eddie that Milton Blackstone had not was to persuade him to improve his knowledge. She introduced Eddie to books, and he became a voracious reader. He became so excited by the discovery of philosophy and ideas he even read Kirkegaard and Nietzsche.

Out of consideration for Connie during her second pregnancy, Eddie tried not to rock the boat. He attempted to stay at home more, sitting up in bed reading and underlining profound statements. But he simply could not sit still for long; his habits had become too ingrained.

In celebration of Connie's August 8th birthday (1968), after her return from Las Vegas, Eddie gave her a surprise party at The Factory, inviting a large number of her friends. But on the night of Eddie's Cocoanut Grove opening, they had a fight, and Eddie was not behaving either considerately or kindly. To show her he didn't care whether she attended his opening or not, he left her to get there the best way she could. When she got to the Grove, she found she had to sit at a table with Steve Brandt.

Eddie's spite went even further a few nights later. Connie attended a performance with a business associate of Eddie's; after dinner they were to meet Eddie in his hotel suite. After his performance, Eddie had been supplied with an attractive redhead by one of his many friends gathered in his suite. The couple disappeared into the bedroom together. One of Eddie's guests saw Connie and Eddie's business associates in the hall, and he rushed into the suite to let Eddie know. However, Eddie pointedly waited until after his wife was inside the suite before he ushered his redheaded guest out of the bedroom.

Connie did not accompany Eddie to Chicago at the end of August when he left to appear at the Democratic National Convention at the request of Chicago Mayor Richard Daley. Some of Eddie's friends did accompany him.

During the late 1960s, the American nation had been torn by violence and divided ideals. The Democratic Convention in Chicago in 1968 became the scene of one of the most terrifying and violent acts of the decade. The nation witnessed on their home television screens what would later be called "a police riot." Young demonstrators had gathered in Chicago to protest against the Vietnam war; they had already succeeded in convincing President Lyndon Johnson not to seek another term in office; they now wanted a promise of peace from the Democratic Party platform.

Mayor Richard Daley ruled Chicago with an iron hand; he was little more than a petty dictator, and he did not approve of the demonstrators in his city. When tempers flared, the Chicago police charged the demonstrators, leaving many of them bleeding and injured. The world was shocked at seeing what had become of the American Dream, and that shock—added to the many other shocks of the Sixties—would seethe beneath the nation's consciousness, eventually prompting the people to demand a return to more humanistic values.

Up in his suite in the Ambassador Hotel, Eddie Fisher and his friends did not care a great deal about what was happening down in the streets. He was meeting rich and powerful people. He was also having a delightful time with a beautiful model for a *Playboy* magazine centerfold. He saw a lot of her in Chicago and at the farm belonging to one of his new wealthy friends near Lake Geneva, Wisconsin. He would also see her in Los Angeles when she came out to do a television show about *Playboy* planned for one of the major networks.

In her second pregnancy within two years, Connie was gaining quite a bit of weight. Eddie felt trapped by his wife's pregnancies, and he was not happy having to face Connie. It was just one more problem on top of all the others that had been bombarding him in the past few years, and he wanted desperately to ignore it.

There was one problem Eddie suddenly found himself facing that he could not ignore: the Internal Revenue Service was questioning him about back taxes he owed. The IRS charged that he owed them $42,153, and he challenged that claim. Milton Blackstone was being investigated by the IRS separately, and he too was contesting. The years in question for Eddie were the lean years of RamRod; the years in question for Milton were the ones when Eddie was married to Elizabeth, when Milton, thus, received no income.

Eddie had to make several trips to New York that fall to try to deal with his income tax problems. When he was there in October, he met an attractive young college student with the first name of

Lucille. She was a pretty twenty-year-old brunette who wore custom-made denim and hippie-type pants outfits. She was an aspiring poet and songwriter, and she had a particular attraction for Eddie because she was not only pretty, but intelligent and well-read. In an effort to impress her, he began reading all the more.

Later that month, Eddie had to go back to Las Vegas for another appearance at the Frontier, and Lucille followed him. While he was onstage, she would sit in his dressing room and write poetry. Eddie would read her work, and then give her his opinions of it, and they would often stay up all night talking.

Unlike the numerous other girls who continued to pass in and out of Eddie's life, Lucille remained his friend for some time. But she did not stay with him in his hotel room; she had her own hotel accommodations.

After the Frontier engagement, when Eddie returned to Los Angeles and to Connie, he again made an effort at being kind to his wife. Connie had been having a difficult time with this pregnancy, and her health was not good. Christmas was coming; it was a family time, and it was important to Connie.

On the morning after Christmas, Eddie took Connie to St. Joseph's hospital in Burbank, where she gave birth to another girl. They gave their second daughter the name Tricia Lee Fisher. Surprisingly, Eddie seemed content to spend time after that with Connie and the two children. But with Eddie, that could not last for long.

While he was in Mexico City in January of 1969, Eddie made a gesture toward giving up some of his wild activities, but Connie did not understand the gesture. He gave away the video tape recorder to a well-known businessman suspected of having connections with the underworld. Connie was furious because she had bought the machine as a gift to help her husband with his career.

Frustrated, Eddie began to see he would never be able to please Connie; he might as well try to please himself. What there was to their marriage was definitely on the rocks. Eddie would later say of Connie, "She's a Valley girl, and she'll always be a Valley girl," meaning presumably that she belongs among the nice homes and the nice family atmosphere of the San Fernando Valley, just over the hills from Hollywood.

Connie herself had some problems now: she had gained almost sixty pounds during her difficult second pregnancy, and she had to lose that weight before her scheduled appearance at the Flamingo in April.

Eddie returned to the Frontier in February, and he also returned to his good times with guests in his dressing room and hotel suite. A new face at the party was a cousin of Elvis Presley, and he too had no difficulty attracting beautiful women to their parties.

During this engagement Eddie met a very intriguing young Swedish girl at a party in Beverly Hills; Connie and Eddie hosted, doing their best to give the impression of marital bliss. She was a tall brunette with a fantastic figure and violet eyes like Elizabeth Taylor's. Her name was Eeda and she had come to the party with a friend of Eddie's who went by the name of Chick. Eddie decided he wanted to see more of Eeda.

The drugs and the dissipated life were affecting Eddie's appearance so severely by this time that people could not help but stare at him. He looked twice his natural age; his face and body appeared bloated, and his complexion was best described as "doughy." He had great dark circles under his eyes, and the wrinkles and lines in his face were increasing. He tried to cover up the fact with makeup, but he didn't succeed. He was well past hiding his secret.

Connie was to open at the Flamingo in Las Vegas on April 3; unexpectedly, Eddie would be competing with her directly across the street at Caesar's Palace.

Eddie had signed an exclusive contract with Caesar's Palace, but he hadn't yet begun appearing for them in Vegas. They had scheduled Celeste Holm in *Mame* to open on April 4, but they canceled the engagement. They called on Eddie to fill in that slot. He had wanted an entirely new show for his opening there, and this was short notice to put together a new act; but Eddie put everything into high gear. He had to have new material and a new look—double-breasted velvet jackets with gold-buttons, bell-bottom trousers, silk scarf at the neck.

Connie left for Vegas on March 31, and Eddie remained behind in Los Angeles. It was his golden opportunity to get to know Eeda. And so Eddie contacted his friend Chick and asked him to bring her to his house. Chick had reservations about Eeda staying with Eddie in his home, but he did as he was asked. (Later Chick commented, "Granted I'm no saint, but what kind of guy is he that will bring another woman into his house and make love to her in the same bed in which he sleeps with his wife?")

Eeda stayed at the house with Eddie until he had to go to Vegas on April 3. Then she rode down with Chick in Eddie's Mercedes and stayed at Chick's home in Vegas, to be on hand for Eddie but not so close as to interfere with Eddie's and Connie's hotel arrangements. However, that set-up changed.

The original plan was for Connie and Eddie to stay in his suite at Caesar's Palace, while the children stayed with their nurse at Connie's suite at the Flamingo; but, after the first weekend, the children were brought over to stay with their parents. Eddie managed to see Eeda between shows to have dinner with her.

He was having difficulty maintaining a regular schedule again. After a few days of attempting this regular life, Eddie was up all night and all morning unable to go to sleep. Finally, at one in the afternoon, he decided to take some sleeping pills. He was unable to wake up for his first show. Guy Marks, the comedian, did an extra 25 minutes, while others tried to rouse Eddie to get him onstage. When he did manage to walk out in front of the audience, he could not get through the lyrics of a single song. The audience angrily walked out demanding a refund. When he could do no better at the midnight show, Caesar's Palace cancelled the engagement and Eddie's contract. As far as they were concerned, Eddie Fisher was through in Las Vegas.

Eddie left Connie and returned home to Los Angeles with Eeda. He had his valet, Willard Higgins, take all of Connie's clothes and all of the babies' things out of the house and put them into the guest house. This was his symbolic way of saying their marriage was over and Eeda was his new woman.

But he quickly had doubts about his Swedish charmer. The second night at home, Eddie decided to throw a party for a few friends. After the guests arrived, Eeda made a phone call and told

Eddie she had to go out for a couple of hours.

Later, Eddie was out in the driveway saying good night to one of his guests when a car pulled up in front, spotted Eddie and sped off up the hill. After the guests left, Eddie decided to wait in a dark corner of the driveway to see if the car would return. It did come back, slow down, and stop. Eddie walked over to the car, looked in, and saw Eeda kissing a man goodnight.

He took her inside the house, and the two of them fought all night. The next morning, he kicked her out. She had no money and no place to stay.

On April 24, Eddie went to see his attorneys about filing for divorce from Connie. She was supposed to fly from Las Vegas to New York for her opening at the Persian room on April 29. Instead, she had to rush to Los Angeles to appear in court to answer Eddie's complaints and file her own complaints against him. When reporters asked for an explanation, Eddie answered, "Connie and I love each other, but we can't stay married." To friends, he said, "I love her, but I can't live with her."

The day that Eddie's mother heard the news, she tried calling her son eight times, but he refused to take her calls.

Eeda came back to Eddie apologetically a few days after he filed for divorce. Their romance continued, but they did not pick up where they had left off. To him, after the incident with the man in the car, she was just another girl.

Early in May, he met someone who did seem to be special—Kim Novak. He met her at a friend's house to talk about the possibility of casting her as Elizabeth in *Paint Your Wagon*. He flipped over her, and mentioned she would be right for a role in another movie property he had, *The Gouffee Case*. He told friends he was in love with her, but his ardor soon cooled when he found out how far away she lived.

As the decade of the 1960s came to a close, Eddie Fisher hit rock bottom. His debts grew larger and larger; he had to sell his two-bedroom cottage. He saw himself going nowhere with drugs. It had been a decade of confusion, of trauma, of lies, and of despair; and all of those strains came together for Eddie as the decade ended.

13. Eddie Who?

The 1970s were the time to pay the piper for at least some of the excesses begun in the 1950s. The nostalgia for the silent days of the Eddie Fisher decade had started in the Sixties as a reaction to the protests and demonstrations of the young. The reactionary mood had begun after the riots at the Democratic Convention in 1968, and it had brought about the election of a president who was—in every way—representative of the 1950s' double-faced god. Richard Nixon stood for "law and order," and a frightening majority of the American public didn't seem to care how he achieved it, as long as they didn't have to take the responsibility. The Fifties' mentality, the dependence upon a strong and all-powerful father figure, had returned by the early 1970s. And the election of Nixon and Agnew did manage to silence the young by driving them into despair.

But the "party" would be over shortly after their second election in 1972, and the piper would have to be paid. The uncovering of lies, duplicity, and downright dishonesty at the very top of the political structure put an end to the kind of presidency that had begun in the Fifties. The biggest story of the decade would be something called "Watergate" which resulted in the resignation of the President of the United States, and the jailing of most of his close associates.

There were attempts to do a truly thorough housecleaning of all of the social ills that had originated twenty years before, but many of those attempts were frustrated. The "Drug Problem" simply became greater and greater. The Federal Government made a scapegoat of cigarette smoking, while protecting the interests of those who would push hard drugs and liquor. Civil rights and individual liberties regardless of sex became bogged down in endless quibbling. And the abuses of big business and industry continued to go unchecked, driving the American economy into its most severe economic state since the Great Depression of the 1930s.

Government support of big business and industry, begun in the wartime Forties and institutionalized in the Fifties, had now become coupled with government support of the poor and the aged in the 1960s. The rich and the powerful could avoid having to pay the tab for these programs, and the full financial responsibility would fall on the American Middle Class, the great Silent Majority. As would befit their Fifties self-concept, this majority remained silent and endured the abuses of their system. Rather than protest, they adapted; wives went out to work so that families would have two wage earners. When families increasingly broke apart after this, it hardly mattered. And when good respectable wage-earning citizens increasingly had to declare personal bankruptcy, it still hardly mattered. The rich were getting richer, the poor were being sustained, and the middle class was getting poorer.

Another group, a group that operated outside the law, could no longer hide the fact that it too was growing rich. The "Mafia," organized crime, became a subject of much public interest in the 1970s. Finding its base in the secretive sale of whatever was illegal—drugs, pornography, prostitution, homosexual bars, murder for hire—the "Mafia" moved into successful and respectable businesses, industries, entertainment, labor unions, and even into politics and government itself by the Seventies. It became an accepted fact that where there was big money, there was the hand of the "Mafia." Where there was money, there was power; and, in many parts of the country, the average American citizen lived in fear of this elusive underworld.

Economic theorists muddled along trying to come to grips with the astonishing combination of inflation and recession, ignoring the anomalies that did not fit into their theoretical approach. Meanwhile, the American people scrimped and saved on the essentials of life, and spent enormous amounts on the nonessentials—on books, records, movies, and entertainment. Increasingly, big promoters, basing their approach on the early efforts of

Milton Blackstone, were able to sell the American people anything and everything they did not want. If there were efforts to restrict "payola" in the music and record business, those efforts never seemed to accomplish anything. Rock promoters and sports promoters were able to play games under the table with "ticket scalpers" and get enormous amounts of money for seats to "pseudo-events." In the 1970s, "Superstars" appeared overnight, and disappeared from public popularity just as rapidly as they appeared.

The country that had clutched "built-in obsolescence" to its heart, now welcomed "disposable culture" just as warmly.

By the early 1970s, nobody cared about a broken-down, washed-out singer named Eddie Fisher. Hardly anybody ever even thought about him, and if anyone did, it was usually to wonder, "Whatever happened to . . .?" And by the late 1970s, if his name was mentioned to anyone under thirty, the response was generally, "Who is he?"

Eddie Fisher began the 1970s in the same way he had ended the 1960s—in oblivion. For almost two years, he completely disappeared from public view; they were the most difficult two years of his life. No longer capable of earning the fantastic amounts he had earned in the Fifties, Eddie still had the power to pull in considerably more than the average American taxpayer and homeowner. However, he was a victim of percentages. The government, of course, always got the biggest bite, but there were also agents and managers, ex-wives, and—in Eddie's case—expensive vices. There was simply no way he could make an income that would be greater than his expenses. It was a situation the average American would have to face a few years later. Eddie faced it in 1970.

He had sunk far over his head into debt. There was no solution but to declare bankruptcy. On August 19, 1970, in Puerto Rico, he testified in U.S. District Court that Edwin Jack Fisher, Eddie Fisher, Eddie Fisher Productions, Fisher Productions, Eddie Fisher Enterprises, and Fisher Enterprises had assets amounting only to $40,000 in municipal bonds held by the Bank of America. He gave as his only place of residence an apartment—Ocean Towers, Apartment 506, San Juan. He was later released from a one-million dollar debt to Warner Brothers from earnings on his nightclub appearances, and he was released from his $1,000 a month child-support payments to Connie Stevens.

The advantage of bankruptcy—wiping out the past to allow a new beginning, a fresh start,—gave Eddie Fisher a second chance. Would he be able to take that second chance and truly make a go of it? After what he had done to destroy his career, would he be able to make a comeback?

He would make every effort, but he would be fighting not only his reputation, but also himself.

For awhile, he had the help of an attractive young woman named Barbara Hayman. Eddie first met Barbara years before, when he had been married to Debbie Reynolds, and she had been married to Fred Hayman, manager of the Beverly Hilton Hotel. When they re-met at a New Year's Eve party in 1970, Barbara was single and free, having been divorced from Hayman and having gone back to UCLA to get her Master's Degree in Psychology. Eddie was also free; his Swedish beauty had left him after he had declared bankruptcy, returning home to Sweden.

Barbara was a pretty, dark-haired, bright-eyed woman in her thirties. She was intelligent, and she was the only Jewish girl Eddie ever got serious about. Still very much attracted to books and ideas, and very concerned about what he considered to be a psychological addiction to drugs, he found Barbara the first girl in some time whose appeal went beyond physical attraction.

Barbara did everything she could, using her background in psychology, to help Eddie in his effort to break his addiction. She also lent him much needed money, and encouraged him to plan his comeback. It seemed that this relationship was making a significant change in Eddie; everyone who came into contact with him noticed it. Even Debbie Reynolds commented publicly in favor of Barbara Hayman.

This was not just a platonic friendship; Barbara was not acting as a doctor or counselor just to help Eddie. She was very much in love with him, and he was in love with her. Eddie began to take better care of himself, exercising and playing tennis every day; and he began to ease away from his dependency on drugs.

He hired a new agent, George "Bullet" Durgom, to take on the virtually impossible task of breaking down the resistance of clubowners to get him appearances. Durgom managed to get Eddie an appearance at the Sahara-Tahoe Hotel in Lake Tahoe for January of 1972 where he did a terrific job, performing his old standards and Al Jolson songs.

Eddie was doing well enough by the spring of 1972 for Durgom to be able to schedule a tour of appearances beginning at the Venetian Room of San Francisco's Fairmont Hotel. On opening night there, he was a little scared. It was a small room; and, when the spotlight appeared on him, he had to walk from the back to the front of the room, where a microphone had been placed on a front table. He looked a little bewildered when the applause started, as if he weren't quite sure anyone had come to see him. He picked up his mike and began, "Let Me Entertain You."

He did not stick with his old standard hits, but did newer more contemporary songs, such as "For the Good Times," in which he harmonized with his accompanist and friend of eighteen years, Eddy Samuels. The audience's warm applause gave him confidence, and he did his Jolson medley. He then paused and remarked, "People always ask me why I don't sing my own songs. I just happen to love Jolson's songs better than all the rest, and I'll sing them as long as I am alive. That man and his songs are part of me." He then got down on one knee, commenting, "This always gets me into trouble—I propose," and sang "Sonny Boy."

After the good audience response, Eddie felt he had made a new beginning. He would have to work his way back up to the big time, gradually regaining the respect of audiences and nightclub managers; he felt it would be worth the effort. He continued his tour around the country, playing the smaller, less important rooms but continuing to improve his image. In August, he went home to Philadelphia to spend his birthday with his family. While he was there, sitting and talking to his father, Joseph Fisher suffered a heart attack and died. Eddie was grief-stricken.

It is difficult to judge whether it was his father's death that affected him, or the fact that Barbara Hayman had talked to the press about how she had "helped" Eddie, but Eddie began to return to his old ways. He became deeply depressed, telling friends, "I have lost all faith in myself." He was losing weight, down from his usual 160 pounds to a weight of 118 pounds.

However, he continued to meet his commitments and to make his appearances.

On November 20, 1972, Eddie—as well as Milton—was hit by a second shock; Jennie Grossinger, after a long illness, died. She was eighty years old.

Milton would still not respond to the pleas of his brothers, Daniel Blackstone and Leo Schwartzstein, to allow them to obtain additional care and professional counsel for him. Two years earlier, in October of 1970, Milton had spent a week at the Bowery's Shelter Care Center for men. When the doctor there recommended he be sent to a hospital for special treatment, Milton had insisted Dr. Jacobson be called. Of course, Jacobson demanded that Milton be sent to him.

Sometime afterward, two policemen apparently thought Milton's actions were abnormal. They picked him up and took him to Bellevue Hospital. In a rage, he again demanded the doctors call Jacobson. Again, he was released in Jacobson's care.

That year, 1970, Milton's brothers started their campaign to save him from his confused state. They began by writing pleading letters to Dr. Jacobson, asking him to explain Milton's problem or advise him to get another opinion. The doctor ignored their pleas, as was his right on the principle of doctor/patient relationship. They next tried the New York Medical Society, but got no response from there either. They did, however, receive a verbal protest from songwriter Alan Jay Lerner, himself a Jacobson patient, telling them in so many words to mind their own business.

After the death of his brother Leo, Daniel Blackstone successfully reached the *New York Times* and asked for assistance with his cause. In early December, after five weeks of investigation, the *Times* exposed Dr. Max Jacobson. The whole sordid story came out into the open, reported by every major newspaper and magazine in the country. Names of his patients were published (including John F. Kennedy and Eddie Fisher); it was revealed that his drugs were mixed in a crude workshop by unpaid and unlicensed volunteers, themselves patients of Jacobson, who could no longer afford to pay for the service. Drugs, needles, and vials were dispensed freely; ninety percent of his patients injected themselves, many suffering hepatitis and other problems from improper care of needles. As a result of the *Times* article, Dr. Jacobson was investigated by the New York State Board of Medicine, and former patients of Dr. Max were called to testify.

Even after this news came out, Milton Blackstone refused to accept anything bad about his doctor and friend. Eddie said nothing publicly. At the request of his brother Daniel, Milton ended his doctor/patient relationship with Jacobson, though their personal relationship remains.

Eventually, the untiring efforts of Daniel Blackstone paid off and he was able to help Milton regain his physical strength and mental ability. Yet, when the "Dr. Feelgood" scandal broke, Milton was still living his life as though he were a spectator instead of a participator.

Eddie was playing the Latin Casino in New Jersey that December when, over Christmas, his health began to deteriorate severely. Frightened, he made plans to go away for a rest.

He flew to Jamaica in January and stayed at the Kingston Hilton with a friend. Eddie was determined to hide out there and break from the drugs "cold turkey." Having failed to ease off them gradually, he had decided this was the only way.

He did not realize how totally dependent his body had become upon them. He had no idea that sudden withdrawal could mean vascular collapse—and death.

The first day was easier than he had anticipated, giving him a false sense of the way it would be, but the following days got rougher and rougher. He suffered his first seizure a few nights after he had begun, collapsing on the floor of his room. He was found unconscious shortly thereafter, and was revived. Then, several nights later, he had a seizure he was not pulling out of.

He was rushed to a hospital in Kingston where he was given only one chance in five of surviving. He was so weak he could not lift his head off his pillow, and he had to be watched day and night. Slowly, he began to improve and to regain his strength.

He hadn't completely recovered when he returned to Los Angeles, but he knew he had to get back to work because he needed money. Thinking he had broken his addiction, he confidently and quickly returned to the drugs, wrongly assuming there would be no repeated dependency.

During the next year, he was in and out of hospitals and clinics trying over and over again to break free of his drugs, each time thinking when he left that he was cured. On one occasion, doctors discovered a lump in his breast, and Eddie feared it might be cancer. But it proved to be benign.

Eddie began to have problems with Barbara Hayman; she could not resist talking to reporters about Eddie, and particularly about how she had helped him in his battle against drugs. He began to fear she was in the relationship for the publicity. He thought she intended to take advantage of the situation to write a book about him.

Finally, in June of 1974, Eddie himself felt he was ready to speak out publicly about his trouble with drugs. Although he was still having to take sleeping pills, he felt he had conquered the problem with the methamphetamines he had been taking.

In November of 1974, Eddie seemed ready for his big comeback. He arranged with his good friend Buddy Hackett to appear with him at the Sahara Hotel in Las Vegas. But when Eddie had to go into the hospital with a liver ailment, he had to cancel. The "comeback" with Buddy was rescheduled for February of 1975 at the Sahara. Eddie underwent plastic surgery to have the bags under his eyes removed, as well as three inches off each side of his face. He worked hard to get himself into shape.

The opening was a success. Accompanied by a twenty-piece orchestra, he was in good form. After the show, warmed by the thunder of applause, Eddie brought Connie Stevens on stage to share the moment with him, setting off rumors that they would be remarried. Unlike as with his other wives, Eddie had settled into a good friendly relationship with Connie, going to see his children whenever possible.

Carrie Fisher in "Star Wars."

Bobby Hall, the murdered private detective.

Buddy Hackett helped Eddie with comeback.

Some newspaper headlines.

Eddie as he was . . .

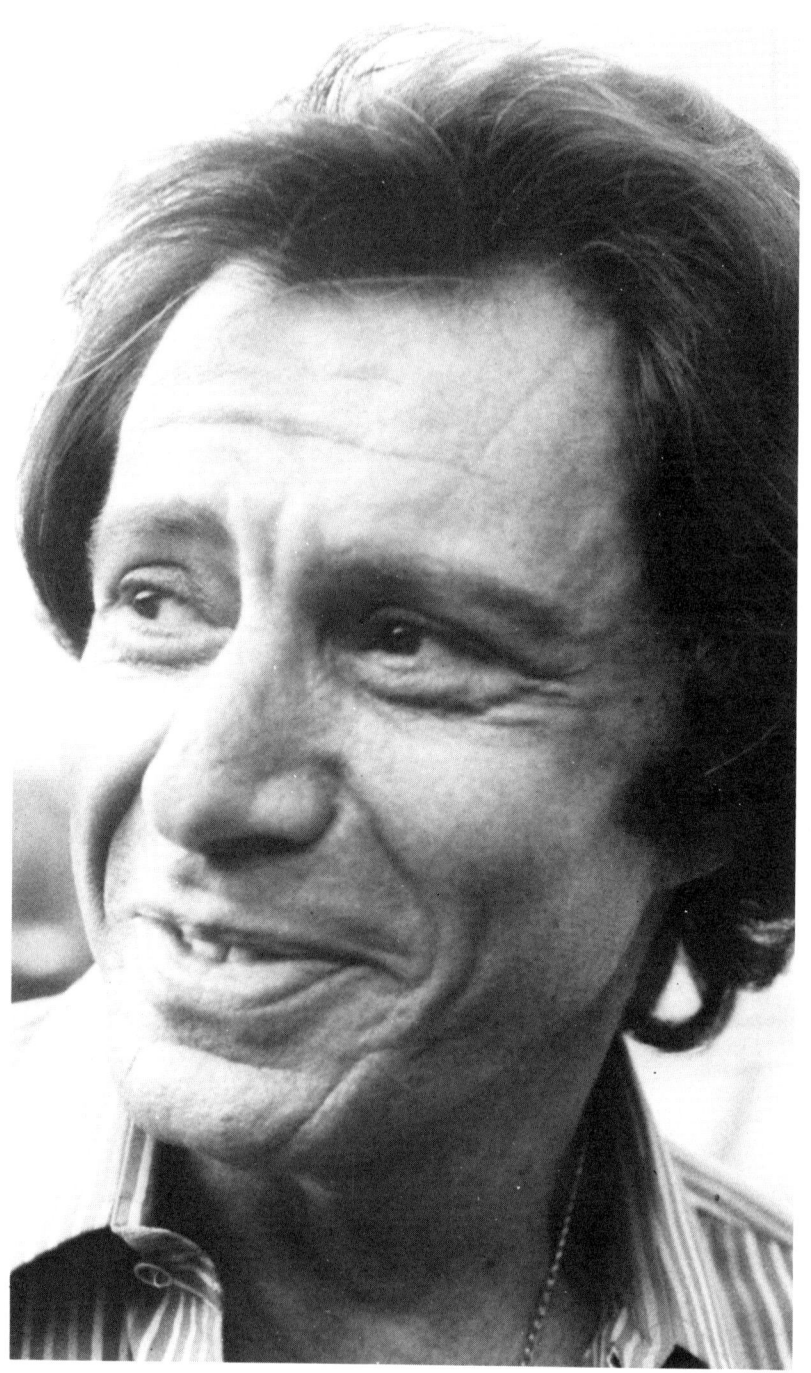

And as he is today.

. . . with Roy Radin's Vaudeville Revue.

Eddie's euphoria was short lived. Soon after the opening, he developed "desert throat," a form of laryngitis. With regrets, Buddy Hackett had to call in a new entertainer, Dick Roman (now deceased), to replace Eddie.

Eddie recovered in time to join Buddy for the remainder of their tour, playing the Valley Forge Music Fair in Pennsylvania and the Westbury Music Fair in New York. Feeling confident about his return to the bigtime, Eddie scheduled some appearances of his own, opening at the Riviera in Las Vegas on June 28 and receiving a standing ovation.

Buoyed with hope that his life was beginning to work again, Eddie went from Vegas to appear at the Concord Hotel, the major rival to Grossinger's in upstate New York. (He had experienced a dispute with Paul Grossinger, and he now declared, "The Concord is my new home.") He appeared at the nearby Monticello Racetrack in August, and then went on to make his first television appearance in six years by co-hosting The Mike Douglas Show for one week in September.

Eddie was naturally nervous about the occasion, but the problems he evidenced on the show did not stem from nerves. His speech was slurred, and his mind wandered when he was telling a story. He was still taking sleeping pills to counteract the sleeplessness that had resulted from dropping methamphetamines. His performance on Mike Douglas hurt any possibilities of his appearing as a guest on other television shows.

During that show, he was asked about his 21-year drug addiction. It was already public knowledge he had been a patient of Dr. Jacobson.

Following the thorough investigation by the *New York Times* and public disclosures by family members of patients, more than 4,000 pages of testimony were brought before a five-member panel of physicians for the New York State Board of Medicine. Former patients of Dr. Jacobson testified the "vitamin" shots they had received contained amphetamines and in some cases, caused addiction and hospitalization.

The case became a long, drawn out one. Dr. Jacobson was represented by Simon Rose of the well-known law firm of Louis

Nizer. Mr. Rose prepared an in-depth defense for his client, who on April 24, 1975 was found guilty of 48 charges of misconduct and one count of fraud, resulting in the loss of his license for "unprofessional conduct."

The Board of Regents charged that Dr. Jacobson had used his own self-styled research foundation (to which Fisher and Blackstone once contributed), the Creative Research Foundation, Inc., to disguise purchases of large quantities of amphetamines, needles and syringes for use by patients. Those who could afford to pay, paid for those patients who couldn't. Fees were $75 an injection, and up.

The report showed that excluding 12 months in 1967, from 1964 until 1972, Jacobson's office bought approximately 463,719 hypodermic needles and 236,646 syringes, or 1,270 needles and 650 syringes a week for distribution.

While all this was being unfolded, Eddie had met a new girl, and he had again fallen deeply in love. He had met Terry Richard at a party in Beverly Hills. A pretty, brown-haired, blue-eyed, twenty-one year old, she had been Miss Louisiana in the 1973 Miss World contest. Eddie was with another girl that night (as usual), but he was watching Terry all evening. "Then our eyes met," he recalls, "and we sent messages to each other. I thought she was beautiful, and I didn't want her to get away."

They dated for two months; then Eddie had to go into the hospital unexpectedly, and he was unable to get word to Terry, who assumed he had walked out on her. Terry went to Las Vegas to stay with her parents, but when she heard that Eddie was out of the hospital and that he had been looking for her, she went back to him.

When Eddie was 18 years old, Marlene Dietrich gave him this advice: "Never marry an actress." What she failed to tell him was that it can also be a mistake to marry someone 26 years younger than yourself.

Eddie and Terry were married on October 29, 1975, in Baja, California. Their marriage lasted only four months, despite all of Eddie's best intentions. He announced to Rona Barrett's television audience that this time he planned to settle down "with a real wife." This was the first woman Eddie had married who was not an actress, so there would be no career conflicts. He was off the most serious of his drugs, and he was determined to reform.

Terry's young age gave Eddie a revived youth. He grew a mustache and goatee, and he began dressing like a man in his twenties—open shirts, amulets around his neck, suede pants, and beaded belts and vests. He looked like an aging hippie, but he was enjoying himself.

Terry, like all of Eddie's wives, expected total devotion. She wanted to go everywhere with him, and she wanted to be with him twenty-four hours a day. Except for his years with Elizabeth, Eddie had never been able to take that.

In February of 1976, he had to go to London to appear with Lorna Luft at the Palladium. While they were in London, Terry walked out on him. Immediately, the press was linking Eddie with European film star, Catherine Deneuve.

During 1976, Eddie undid many of the things he had worked so hard to accomplish. After Terry left him, he returned to his erratic partying schedule, rapidly acquiring the haggard look he had so recently corrected with plastic surgery. As during the days of Dr. Jacobson, his surgeon traveled with him for the next several months.

Buddy Hackett again asked Eddie to appear with him at the Sahara in Las Vegas during August. The reviews were good, but Eddie again developed throat problems from the dry Vegas air. Despondently, Eddie had to exit, and the Sahara arranged for Charo to take his place. Before Eddie left, Buddy went out and bought an expensive turquoise-studded belt and a beautiful watch to give to him for his forty-eighth birthday on August 10. As his way of expressing affection, Buddy had the watch engraved, "With Hate, Buddy."

Eddie received his notice of cancellation on the day after his birthday. That evening, when Hackett went on stage for his act, he began to explain to the audience that Eddie was having to cancel because "his throat's been a little rough."

Suddenly, Eddie stormed on stage and shouted, "I do not need an explanation from you. They do not need an explanation because you're going to lie anyway."

Buddy Hackett appeared dumbfounded. He protested honestly, "Eddie, I have never lied in my life."

Eddie screamed back, "You always lie. You're the biggest liar I ever met."

Buddy continued to try to be conciliatory, "Eddie, I'm sorry you're so sick."

The exchange continued back and forth for several minutes, and finally Eddie concluded by taking off the watch Buddy had given him and throwing it at him, shouting, "You can take this watch and shove it!"

Apparently Eddie had blamed Buddy for the cancellation. However, it had come from the Sahara management, and Eddie knew as well as anyone the harm that could come from his trying to continue to sing with a bad throat. Later, it was rumored that the real reason for Eddie's anger was because he thought Buddy was trying to make it with his replacement. Whatever the reason, Eddie seemed to have a knack for cutting his own throat. The Vegas hotels again considered him a high risk.

Way back when Eddie Fisher was a baby, there were two conflicting attitudes toward what America was all about. One said it was security, offering "a chicken in every pot, a car in every garage." The other said it was frankness, vigor, and courage, proclaiming, "the only thing we have to fear is fear itself." That choice was not truly made until the 1950s, and what the American public chose was not the traditional values of courage and honesty and openness because they were afraid of their own shadow. They chose security, what had now become a steak on every barbecue, two cars in every carport.

That choice was not made by the generation that made up the Eddie Fisher fans; it was a choice forced upon them by their parents, who had suffered through depression, world war, and the fear-mongering of anti-communists. The Eddie Fisher generation tried to rebel against this choice, tried to protest against inequality, against undeclared wars, and against the encroachment of materialism. But, by the 1970s, that generation had battle fatigue. They had won some skirmishes against silence and security, but they had not won the war. And they had grown cynical as a result.

They had forsaken vulnerability, honesty, and openness, just as Eddie Fisher had forsaken those qualities. Although they had taken different paths to the same end, Eddie Fisher and his audience had finally come to fear insecurity.

However, late in the 1970s, there was a brief ray of hope. The year 1976 was the Bicentennial Year. The American Dream was two hundred years old, and the Twentieth Century had passed the three-quarters mark. For many people it was a time for reassessment. It was also an election year, and there was a great determination among the people to have their country returned to them. They rejected all of the well-known candidates for president, because they stood for lies, corruption, and compromise. Instead they chose a relatively unknown man named Jimmy Carter who promised only honesty and a good effort to set the country back on its intended course. He was also about as vulnerable a man as a politician could be.

And there were rays of hope on other fronts as well. Among the multitude of motion pictures that offered exploitation and sensationalism, a few began to creep in that offered sensitivity, feeling, honesty, and truth—movies such as *The Turning Point* and *Julia*—and the public responded. A bit of truth and honesty even crept into television, though one of the more sensitive shows, *James at 16*, rapidly ran into trouble with the fearful and protective television executives.

The music and recording business, however, held firmly to their belief that they had the right to sell the public what it did not want. With Eddie Fisher, Milton Blackstone had taught younger promoters how to sell talent; the younger promoters had taken his concepts and refined them into an ability to sell anything at all. Talent had become the least important quality for an entertainer; showmanship could outdo honesty, sensitivity, and truth any day. The promoters of groups such as KISS and The Sex Pistols readily admitted this publicly; what their audiences wanted was hype and noise and excitement—thrills rather than enjoyment.

And they could succeed because they were appealing to a new generation of teenagers, a generation that had been brought up without ever being allowed to know love or honesty or gentleness or sensitivity or vulnerability at all. It was a generation born long after the Fifties had ended, a generation born outside the Garden of Eden, so to speak. They had eaten of the fruit of television and had been forced out into a hyped-up violent materialistic world as soon as they could walk and talk and comprehend. Their buying power did not offer an encouraging future for the things the War Babies had tried to accomplish.

But the War Babies still constituted the largest generation ever to grow up in America, and they still had the greatest "buying power" of any single age group. In the late 1970s, despite KISS and The Sex Pistols, there was a great surge of record sales for some of the stars of the Fifties and early Sixties. There was also a turning to Country and Western where there remained a vestige of truth and honesty and sensitivity.

There was yet some hope.

It was hope, combined with faith, that enabled Milton Blackstone to put his life back together again so that today he enjoys a tranquil, dignified life. He has also re-established his friendships with many of his former friends and colleagues, including Paul Grossinger.

Eddie was not so fortunate for again his name appeared in the papers in an unpleasant light. On July 22, 1976, one of Eddie's former drug buddies, a private investigator named Robert Hall, had been murdered in his Burbank home. In September, Eddie was called in and questioned about Hall. He was only one of a number of celebrities questioned, and the police pointedly told the press that he was not in any way involved in the murder; it was nevertheless unpleasant for Eddie at this critical time in his "comeback," especially when it was leaked that the police had been shadowing Eddie for the past two years because of his drug habits.

After this, Eddie was frequently ill, and his appearances became sporadic.

Eddie did, however, have one thing to be extremely proud of: his daughter Carrie had grown up, and she was becoming a major new star. She had a fine singing voice, and Eddie claimed she was an even better singer than he had been. She had begun her career, appearing with her mother, Debbie Reynolds, in *Irene* and in Debbie's nightclub act. She had gone on from that to a role in the movie *Shampoo,* and then to stardom in the big hit of 1977, *Star Wars.*

His son Todd, Eddie was proud to say, was brilliant, a genius. A very studious boy, and a very shy boy, he would probably make his way behind the scenes instead of onstage or onscreen before the public. He is especially involved in the electronics of sound and recording.

It was good to feel pride in his children. But Eddie also had to feel pride in himself. At age 50, he has been on and off the comeback trail for more than sixteen years. Those attempts to come back had been self-conscious, almost apologetic, almost mocking himself. He had avoided the songs that had taken him to the top, the songs that reminded everyone of the sweet and innocent Eddie Fisher, an Eddie Fisher who obviously didn't exist any longer. Instead, he had tried to sing more contemporary songs, and he had gone back to all the songs that were identified with Al Jolson. He had made jokes about himself and about his mistakes. He told how Dean Martin once quipped, "The reason I drink so much is because when I'm sober, I think I'm Eddie Fisher." Those jokes had gone on for so long, it was possible that even Eddie Fisher thought he was a joke, and nothing more.

After getting Milton Blackstone out of his life, neither Eddie nor anyone else knew how to reproduce his success. The problem was that Eddie Fisher never really knew who he was or what he had that was so good. Aside from an instrument that allowed him to belt out a song without the assistance of tricks or gimmicks, Eddie, like everybody else, thought it was sweetness and innocence, the "boy-next-door" quality. It is true he had that, but that was only the surface quality; the deeper quality was something called vulnerability—the willingness to be open to life. "I felt a terrific need to be liked; I wanted to be known as a nice guy," he now confesses. Eddie crooned of deeply personal things, in intimate tones that suggested he was singing directly to the listener alone. He was leaving himself open to suffer the pain and hurt of rejection.

Ultimately, he was rejected, and he did suffer from it, saying,

"I learned that secretly most of the men I knew hated my guts. I was married to Reynolds, Taylor and Stevens—not to mention the girls I didn't marry . . . and guys wanted to know what the hell I had that they didn't."

Trying to guard himself from further rejection, he continued to make jokes about himself, laughing at himself before anyone else could, refusing to show how truly vulnerable he still was.

Very few performers have been willing to go back again and again showing their true feelings, baring their souls to their publics, despite hurt and rejection; but they were the truly great ones, the truly honest ones. It may be that Judy Garland was the last of that breed. Eventually her vulnerability killed her because she was maintaining it in an age when it was extinct everywhere else. Or at least covered over and hidden behind a cold or brusque veneer.

Honesty, openness, and vulnerability were among the American people's finest qualities. They were the qualities that made us vigorous and kind and loving of our neighbors. And they were the qualities we secretly long for when we look back to another time, superficially recalling the styles, the stars, the movies, the songs. They were the qualities that the 1950s did their level best to destroy, or at least to hide behind sophistication, behind cold intellectualism, and behind a sick, self-mocking humor.

In the Sixties and Seventies, anyone who persisted in remaining honest, open, and vulnerable was immediately labelled a fool. Anyone with a positive outlook had to be stupid. Anyone with a negative outlook was automatically cool and shrewd and had to know what was happening.

Some hope still remains for Eddie Fisher; it may be slight, but it is there. He has tried to make a comeback, time and time again. He has tried to fit in with what he thought his audiences wanted, ridiculing himself, laughing at his mistakes, ignoring who he was, to try to be who he thought the public thought he was.

He continues, weak, escaping through periods of deep depressions. His heart seems to have become calloused; he still seems not to have learned that happiness is a "do-it-yourself" project. After all he has gone through (including an on-again, off-again live-in reconciliation with his fourth wife), he is no longer innocent; but he does remain shy and boyish. Most of all, he continues to be extremely vulnerable. His libido and ego still seem to be in competition with each other. He continues to crave a woman by his side, especially before and after a performance.

Eddie now claims, "Survival is my philosophy, and I believe in love. I don't like people, I like individuals. I like audiences." He begins each performance by saying he is there to sing his heart out. And it seems that for Eddie Fisher, with that right arm raised high, head cocked almost against his left shoulder, eyes closed, only singing can bring true happiness.

The true challenge to Eddie Fisher is finally to grow up and assume the responsibilities in life his audiences have had to assume. Those same people want him to stop hiding from himself with drugs, women and groupies. They want him to face reality with strength and courage, and while he continues his attempt to become a "famous somebody" again, his audiences want him to become a somebody worth being.

Index

"A Man Chases a Girl," 98, 100, 102
Akst, Harry, 95, 98
Ameche, Don, 12, 70
Ann-Margaret, 152
"Around The World in 80 Days," 122
Arthur Godfrey Talent Scouts, 47
Ashman, Eddie, 45

Barrett, Rona, 71, 195
Beat Generation, 6, 127
Beatles, The, 157
Beatniks, 6
Bennett, George, 13, 14, 15, 109, 110
Benny, Jack, 67, 86
Berle, Milton, 55, 64
Billboard, 59
Bill Miller's Riviera, 56-58; 78
Blackstone Agency, The, 41, 42, 130
Blackstone, Daniel, 170, 186-187
Blackstone, Mrs. Daniel, 170
Blackstone, Milton, 12, 15, 16, 18, 40-44; 48, 52, 53, 54-59; 62-68; 69-72; 82, 93, 96, 98-100; 103, 105-106; 118-121; 123, 124, 125, 130, 135, 140, 141, 144, 149-160; 171, 174, 176, 183, 186-187, 198, 200
Boeck, Renata, 152
Boone, Pat, 6
Brandt, Steven, 174-175

Brynner, Yul, 16
"Bundle of Joy," 116, 120-121
Burkhard, Paul, 82
Burstein, Rona—*see* Barrett
Burton, Richard, 147-148; 149-151; 153, 155-156
Burton, Sybil, 155
Butterfield 8, 139, 140, 145

Cantinflas, 122
Cantor, Eddie, 11, 25, 34, 54-55; 73, 92, 112, 141, 145-146
Carter, Jack, 64
Carter, Jimmy, 198
Cash Box, 81
Cat on a Hot Tin Roof, 133
Champion, Marge and Gower, 131
Charo, 196
Churchill, Winston, 18
Cleopatra, 142-143; 145, 146-147; 149, 150, 153
Coca Cola, 67-68; 117, 119
Cocoanut Grove, 83, 85, 86, 145, 152, 174, 175
"Coke Time," 12, 70-71; 80, 81, 82, 83, 90, 93, 101, 119
"Colgate Comedy Hour," 55
Como, Perry, 12, 45, 68, 70, 81
Concord Hotel, 194
Copacabana, 38-40; 43, 45-46; 52, 70, 71, 74
Corey, Jill, 80
Creative Research Foundation, 195
Curtis, Tony, 136

Daley, Mayor Richard, 175
Damone, Vic, 12
Davis, Sammy, Jr., 146
Dawes, Skipper, 30-32; 36, 39-40
Dean, James, 9
Delmont Laboratories, 144
DeMille, Cecil B., 16
Democratic National Convention, 175

Deneuve, Catherine, 196
Dietrich, Marlene, 16, 195
"Dr. Feelgood"—*see* Jacobson, Dr. Max
Domino, Fats, 6
Duke of Edinburgh, 100
Durgom, George "Bullet," 185

Eddie Fisher at the Winter Garden, 153
Eddie Fisher Enterprises, 183
Eddie Fisher Productions, 183
Eeda, 178-180
Eisenhower, Dwight D., 81
Essex House, 81
Estrada, Judge Arcadio, 156
Etess, Mrs. Elaine, 107
Evans, Bob, 171, 172

Ferrer, Mel, 136
Fisher, Alvin "Bunny," 75, 151-152
Fisher, Carrie Francis, 120-121; 125, 133, 141, 169, 189, 199-200
Fisher, Debbie—*see* Reynolds, Debbie
Fisher, Eileen, 89-90
Fisher Enterprises, 183
Fisher, Janet, 91-92
Fisher, Joely, 164, 169, 171
Fisher, Joseph, 21-29; 35, 75, 133, 185
Fisher, Kate, 21-29; 35, 51-52; 75, 89-92
Fisher, Todd Emmanuel, 123-124; 125, 133, 141, 169, 200
Fisher, Tricia Lee, 169, 177
Foreman, Joey, 11, 13, 29-31, 36, 38, 43, 56-58
Frings, Kurt, 151
Froman, Jane, 15, 64, 74, 92
Furies, The, 49
Future Productions, 158

Gobel, George, 119
Goldbogen, Avram—*see* Todd, Mike

Gouffee Case, The, 180
Grant, Johnny, 84
Gregory, Dick, 153
Grossinger's, 12, 13, 40-45; 52, 53-55; 69, 92, 105-110; 119, 130, 131, 140, 152, 158, 159, 194
Grossinger, Elaine—*see* Etess.
Grossinger, Harry, 130
Grossinger, Jennie, 34, 41-42; 107-108; 117, 130, 141, 152-153; 155, 157, 158, 159, 186
Grossinger, Paul, 41, 55-56; 107-109; 141, 159, 194, 199
Grossinger, Tania, 44
Growing Up at Grossinger's, 44

Hackett, Buddy, 164, 188, 189, 194, 196-197
Hall, Robert "Bobby," 189, 199
Halperin, Joseph, 164
Hawaiian Eye, 162
Hayman, Barbara, 166, 184, 186, 188
Hayman, Fred, 184
Heisig, Maria, 143
Higgins, Willard, 179
Hitzig, Dr. William, 14, 15
Holm, Celeste, 178
Hopper, Hedda, 86, 132
House of Wax, 11
Hughes, Howard, 173

Internal Revenue Service, 176
Irene, 200
Irving, Cal, 46

Jacobson, Dr. Max, 16, 17-19; 73, 83, 94, 108, 119, 141, 144, 150-151; 153, 156, 159, 172, 186-187; 194-195
James, Joni, 12
Jessel, George, 55, 146
Johnson, Jeanette, 106-110
Johnson, Lyndon, 176

Jolson, Al, 25, 28, 164, 172, 185, 200
Jolson, Mrs. Al, 95

Kennedy, Jacqueline, 16, 151
Kennedy, John F., 16, 141, 151, 155, 157, 187
Korean "Civil War," 59-68
Khrushchev, Nikita, 136

LaRosa, Julius, 16
Leigh, Janet, 136
Lerner, Alan Jay, 16, 71, 171, 172, 186
Lewis, Jerry, 86, 146
Lincoln Foundation, 144
Loos, Anita, 122
Lucille, 177
Luft, Lorna, 196
Lyons, Leonard, 155

MacCrae, Gordon, 83
Mager and Mager, 118
Mame, 178
Mann, Harvey, 153
Marks, Guy, 174, 179
Martin, Dean, 146, 200
MCA, 120
Mike Douglas Show, 163, 194
Mills Brothers, 49
Moiseyev Dancers, 136, 145
Monroe, Marilyn, 9, 16
Montgomery, Mr. and Mrs. George, 78—*see also* Shore, Dinah
Morrow, Buddy, 32, 33, 34
Moscow Film Festival, 145

New York Times, The, 58, 59, 64, 136, 186-187; 194
Night of the Iguana, The, 156
Nizer, Louis, 194-195
Novak, Kim, 180

Nussbaum, Rabbi Max, 134

"Oh, My PaPa," 82, 168
Oklahoma, 34

Paint Your Wagon, 171, 180
Palladium, 13, 67, 72-73; 97-100; 196
Paramount Pictures, 171
Paramount Theatre, 11, 12, 13, 14, 15, 48-49; 52, 59, 60, 68, 69, 75
Parsons, Louella, 95, 125-126
Pasternak, Louis, 83
Peep Show, 121
Pesin, Lenore, 44
Pet Milk Company, 30
Philip, Duke of Edinburgh, 100
Pius XII, Pope, 18
Porter, Cole, 101
Powers, Stephanie, 152
Preminger, Otto, 16
Presley, Elvis, 6, 104, 120, 157, 178
Princess Margaret, 72-73; 77
Proser, Monte, 39-40; 42, 43, 45, 52, 70, 82, 153
Prowse, Juliet, 153

Queen Elizabeth, 72, 100
Quinn, Anthony, 16

RamRod Productions, 118-119; 141, 154-155; 158
Ray, Johnnie, 12
RCA Building, 71
RCA Victor, 55, 56, 57, 58, 67
Reynolds, Debbie, 80, 81, 83-135; 166, 184, 200, 201
Rich, Bernie, 11, 13, 29-32, 36, 38, 56-58
Richard, Terry, 167, 195-196
Riviera Club—*see* Bill Miller's Riviera
RKO-Radio Studios, 120
Robbins, Fred, 70

Rockefeller, Nelson, 16
Roman, Dick, 194
Romoff, Colin, 136
Rose, Simon, 194-195
Roy Radin's Vaudeville Revue, 193

Saint, Eva Marie, 130
Salk, Dr. Jonas, 16
Samuels, Eddy, 185
Sarnoff, Robert, 67
Schwartzstein, *see* Blackstone, Milton and Daniel
Schwartzstein, Leo, 159, 186
Shaknow, Jane, 72
Shampoo, 200
Shore, Dinah, 12, 67-68; 78, 86
Simon Gratz High School, 32
Simon, Neil, 162
Sinatra, Frank, 11, 31-32; 45, 48-49; 53, 56, 63, 146, 152, 153, 171
Stacy, James, 162, 163
Star Spangled Girl, The, 162, 164
"Star Wars," 189, 200
Spellman, Francis Cardinal, 77
Stevens, Connie, 161-180; 184, 188, 201
Stordahl, Axel, 12
Styne, Jules, 173
Suddenly Last Summer, 135, 142
Sullivan, Ed, 12

Tammy, 120
Tannen, Judy, 71
Tate, Sharon, 174
Taylor, Elizabeth, 80, 121, 122, 123, 124-125; 128-156; 162, 163, 166, 176, 196, 201
Taylor, Mara, 122, 135
Todd, Christopher, 124
Todd, Liza, 123, 137, 143

Todd, Mike, 42, 117, 121-125; 129, 131, 132-133; 134, 135, 137, 140, 153
Todd, Mike, Jr., 124, 135, 151
Truman, Harry, 64-65

USA CANTEEN, 64, 74
U.S. Army Band, 63-64
USO, 103

Variety, 85, 155
Ventura, Charlie, 38

Warren, Fran, 57
Weaver, Pat, 67
Weitman, Bob, 42, 48, 52, 59
Welkes, Danny, 130
Werblin, Sonny, 70
Wilding, Michael, 80, 143
Williams, Tennessee, 16, 135
Wilson, Earl, 130
Wynn, Joan, 46-48; 49, 55-56; 80, 167

"You Gotta Have Heart," 102